Tails to Tell

By Irene Sowter

Tudor Press (London),
27, Old Gloucester Street,
London, WC1N 3XX.

First published 1992

Copyright © Irene Sowter

All rights reserved. No portion of this book may be reproduced or utilised in any form or by any means, electronic or mechanical, including photocopying, recording or retrieval system, without the prior permission in writing of the author, Irene Sowter. Nor is it to be otherwise circulated in any form or binding or cover other than that in which it is published.

ISBN 1 874514 02 X

Printed and typeset by The Longdunn Press Ltd,
Barton Manor, St Philips, Bristol BS2 0RL.

CONTENTS

	Page
INTRODUCTION	5

Chapter

1	My Spiritual Healing Gift	7
2	Charlie Kemp Arrives	13
3	Spiritual Operational Contact Healing	34
4	Training Behind the Scenes	43
5	The Painted Lady	54
6	What I Believe	85
7	"Patients' " Cures	91
8	Billy Boy	95
9	No Card Needed	114
10	With All God's Creatures	152
11	Animals Guided	170
12	"Seek and Ye Shall Find"	175

Dedication

I dedicate this book to my husband, Gerald, for his loving care, encouraging support and sound advice.

Introduction

THE contents of this book constitute a true account regarding the power of spiritual healing for animals, and the psychic and spiritual events which occurred in the very early part of my life.

I would like to point out that being a very practical and down-to-earth person, I am not given to flights of fantasy into a dream world. Moreover, I have never had the time just to sit and dream.

Without question, there will be those who are sceptical of psychic and spiritual phenomena. Well, so be it. That is their prerogative.

I have related the facts of some of my childhood's psychic and spiritual experiences as I lived through them and know them to be to the present day.

Under no circumstances do I intend to try to convert anyone to my way of thinking regarding life beyond the veil for all, by using their free will, must find their own level of understanding on these matters.

But I sincerely trust that readers of my book will be given some food for thought, especially regarding the tremendous healing power of the natural healing energies. Who knows, they might discover within themselves a latent gift of healing? This may spur them on to seek and develop their own healing talents for the benefit of countless numbers of poor, sick animals in our appalling and frightening world of today. I refer to all God's living creatures in need.

All the stories quoted in this book are based upon genuine testimonials. Please note, though, that in some cases pseudonyms have been used. Additionally, where permission has been granted for accounts to appear, the owner's surname has been attached to that of the pet as we definitely consider them to be members of the family . . . and should always be treated as such.

Irene Sowter

"MAN'S many gifts endowed to him at birth, countless as the signs that point his chosen course, yet none more precious in his span on earth than that his hands are guided by the healing source.
"Though man stands dominant among all living things, give thought to creatures of the forest and the air. Their birthright equals man's love, much pleasure brings they too have need, the healing gift to share."

"Divine Spirit may all people use this wondrous gift that knows no prejudice of class or race or creed, inspire their minds to serve that ever they uplift all souls to comfort by their every word and deed."

Denis Hotton

Chapter 1

My Spiritual Healing Gift

MY healing mission began to develop – I remember so clearly – when I was about three years old.

People, especially the poor, showed more care for one another in the earlier part of this century. If any of the neighbours were unfortunately taken ill, as often was the case, my beloved mother would always be one of the first on the scene to offer comfort and help by taking along bowls of hot soup, which she made out of two-penny worth of meat bones. I shall never forget those bones – some big, some small – because I loathed them as they were parts of dead bodies. To thicken the soup, mother would add a carrot or two, turnips and some barley.

As I grew older, my young brother and I had to stand in the queue (which always seemed to me a mile long) at the butchers in Portobello Road, West London, to get the bones every Saturday night as there was a great demand for them, especially where we lived. If the butcher was feeling generous, he would throw in some left over faggots and sausages as well, quite often for one penny. Unbelievable? It happened more than once. One night we were frozen stiff and thinking of leaving the queue to go home when I felt a spirit hand on my shoulder. A lady's voice said: "Do not leave. The butcher is kindly disposed towards children, more so when they look hungry." After that I used to stick it out whether it rained or snowed. No wonder mum used to be so pleased when we were able to give her lots of goodies.

However, my mother always seemed to have the soup ready in times of emergencies. She was forever helping those in need as best she could. Unbeknown to her, I am sure spirit friends were nudging her so she would be prepared in advance when calls for help came. I was never left behind and had to go with her, which pleased me very much since I loved the visits. They gave me the opportunity to climb onto the sick one's bed. Whether they were men, women or children, I always felt an invisible, very friendly presence pushing and propelling, sometimes lifting me up towards them.

On occasions I would see a small group of spirit people with two or three children with them. As I was so young, I accepted them and used to say "Hello." When I did not see them, I used to ask my mother where they were. At first, before she realised what was happening, she looked all round the neighbour's rooms, even under their beds. Then she would go out of the rooms and back again. When patients asked what she was looking for, my poor mother had no answer to give them. She was not amused.

But soon afterwards when we had further visits to make she would always, before we entered the premises, stand in front of me and look down with a finger to her lips. I had to keep quiet. Now, I can see how funny those incidents were and explained the puzzled expressions on the patients' faces at the time.

I would feel an overwhelming urge just to touch them. I remember experiencing every time a wonderful feeling of upliftment and extreme happiness when I did so: the rooms always seemed to light up and glow. I was far too young to understand why I should act in this way. My parents could not, and certainly did not give the matter a second thought. No-one took any notice of me as I sat as quiet as a mouse, just touching the sick person.

Looking back to those days, it did appear that some in need of healing had an idea of what was taking place for when mother thought I had sat on the beds long enough, she would say: "Come along, Irene. Stop being a pest." Many would reply: "Mrs Clements, please let Irene stay. I feel better when she touches me." Reluctantly I would move away and climb down, being aware of the burning heat in my hands and hearing some of those I had touched exclaim they had felt very hot and a lot of heat was coming from me to them.

It did not make any difference since no-one, including my parents at that time, and, during the following years, understood my healing gift – least of all myself.

Not only did I want to touch humans, but sick animals as well. It was not until I reached my early teens that I began to realise what it meant, a slow awakening to what lay ahead for me.

Gradually, from time to time in my childhood days, the doors of spiritual healing for animals were opened to me. When creatures that were ill happened to cross my pathway, I would place my hands on them. Some were cured of their ailments or received improvement whilst others showed no benefit. Healers are like the members of the veterinary and medical professions and others who work in the fields of complementary medicines. We all have our failures. None of us is perfect. If we were, there would not be a single ill person or animal in the entire world.

As a spiritual healer of many years long standing – and blessed still to be in action – I have always been aware only of the power of God's love in existence, and the peace and harmony which transcends through the presence of those from the spirit world who come to teach and work with me for the benefit of man, the animal, bird and all of His kingdoms. The healing energies come from the God head, the supreme, divine being, the source of all light.

Like other healers, I cannot say exactly how these healing energies work. I do not know. But they certainly work. Witness the blind, the deaf, the crippled, the seriously ill, and animals receiving in many cases instant cures or improvements. Well then, there is no denying whatsoever the existence of the natural spiritual healing power. Neither can I ever deny the existence of our beloved spirit vet, the doctors and their colleagues who reside in the beautiful world of light for they all make our healing – I work with my husband – what it is today.

Normally, I experience great heat emanating from my hands when giving healing to creatures (human or otherwise) during the course of treatment. Sometimes the temperature varies. It is most interesting and enlightening. I have noticed it can change whereby the palms of my hands are very hot and my fingers quite cold, or one hand cool, the other warm. Patients often remark on the difference. This is how I work: my husband also works in similar vein. Of course, I cannot speak for other healers.

When I start to give healing – having meditated and prayed to God for those seeking help, and sending out my thoughts for guidance to my spirit friends beforehand – I then become aware of light moving towards me. I know the dear team of spiritual healers are drawing close for me to act as their conductor so that the healing energies can function and transmit energy for contact treatment to commence.

Then I feel the pulsating energy surging through my hands onto the one in need, whether it be an animal or a human. I am extremely uplifted and completely relaxed in the knowledge that no harm will come to them . . . or to me either!

I feel as though an electric current has been switched on. The length of time during the healing sessions (and we see each patient separately) can vary considerably from two, three, four or five minutes to half an hour, sometimes an hour. My dedicated spirit healers do not work to time; they do not watch clocks. What a blessing! When they are going to stop, I become aware of the healing balm withdrawing from my hands, then we attend to the next patient.

I know there are healers who say they work to a specific five minutes. So be it. How they work is their own business. But I cannot work like that. I prefer to leave timing to those that know best – the wise ones beyond the veil.

There are some organisations who prefer to teach pupils a certain way of healing by their methods. To me, with all respect, this is rather like a standard production line; fledgling healers are all coming off a conveyor belt, stamped with the same design, running in the same line of action. I feel that this is a pity for in some cases their individuality and potential healing capabilities are cramped and stifled by the disciplines set before them. Of course, healers need to study and learn the basic elements of spiritual healing, but they should be allowed to breathe and expand their abilities within reason, especially when they possess the direction and spiritual guidance to do so. In other words, healers should hold themselves at liberty to exercise their own impressions. Spiritual healers, like other mediums/sensitives, are all individuals just the same as their spirit inspirers who have their own individual approaches. Those inspirers, by working in attunement with their earth channels, can notice those with remarkable healing qualities and can therefore bring them to the utmost fruition in their own individual way for the benefit of mankind.

If I had listened to restrictive rules and regulations laid down by those, no doubt of good intent, and not to my beloved spirit inspirers, I definitely would not have achieved the stage of my spiritual healing development in which I am privileged to work. These are my views, but we all have the right to draw our own conclusions.

The healing energies, like the spirit world, are not a new commodity. They have always been there and available to man as part of his natural heritage. It is a pity he has not looked at them more closely. Animals are extremely aware of their existence.

The Spirit says, "To date, the divine healing power is not being used to its fullest extent." But in time to come, healers from the other side of the curtain, if given the opportunity and the availability of the right earth channels – whom I trust will not be afraid to stand up and be counted regarding their work as healers – will show the world the greatness and wonder of God's healing energies. This shall bring to millions of people cures of many "incurable" diseases for vast stocks of healing agencies in the world of the spirit are waiting to be tapped and harnessed, to be used by mankind in so many different ways.

One of these is spiritual operational healing in which my husband Gerald and I work together as a team in this particular field of healing. We are delighted to be amongst the forerunners in this country. Regarding this work, we feel there must be many other healers who could work likewise, but perhaps they are afraid of ridicule. This does happen, more's the pity. And the brickbats always come from the unenlightened.

Regarding spirit operational healing for animals, we work with our spirit vet, Charlie Kemp, of whom I shall tell more later I am entranced by him for this form of healing, but not unconscious as it is only a light state of trance. I am aware of Charlie being extremely close to me as he uses my hands for operational and other healing.

At this point, I would like to mention before anyone arrives at the wrong conclusion that at no time are any surgical instruments used by us. No incisions are made in any way at all. The animals are not caused any distress or discomfort when Gerald, Charlie and myself work together.

Now I will move on to relate the wonderful, uplifting effect the power of spiritual healing has in every way on these dear creatures.

It is a great pleasure for us to give healing to them. They bring such love, trust and understanding into our centre and – dare I say it – more so than some humans. All creatures being psychic, they thoroughly enjoy receiving healing. In fact, many times, regardless of how ill they happen to be, they become so relaxed, peaceful and content that they often fall fast asleep under our hands – and we certainly do not use any anaesthetics to bring that about!

In the "Pet's Corner" within our sanctuary, I always know in advance when Charlie Kemp, accompanied by his beloved companion Spot, the dog, is on his way, long before I see them arrive. Suddenly, dogs will look up, wag their tails, give a little bark and smile whilst cats purr in greeting. They wait lovingly for Charlie to touch them, secure in the knowledge that he will not hurt them in any way. Neither will Spot.

People often tell us that their pets instinctively know the day and time they are going to visit us for healing. They become very excited, and run backwards and forwards to the door and cannot get out of the house and into the car fast enough. When they arrive near to our building – sometimes it can be two or three roads away – they know exactly where they are. Then the fun starts, and the animals become more excited and try to leave their car as soon as possible. With due respect to the veterinary profession, we are so informed that this kind of behaviour is not evident when animals have to visit them.

We have so often seen dogs and cats come rushing through the centre door leaving their masters and mistresses behind, making a bee-line straight into the animal healing sanctuary. In their eagerness and enthusiasm, they often try and jump the queue. They are certainly very aware and appreciative of the spiritual benefits, and see and hear Charlie and Spot, who loves to welcome them.

Now I have set the pattern, giving an insight into our animal healing work with Charlie Kemp and Spot, I will continue, and trust readers will be given further food for thought.

Chapter 2

Charlie Kemp Arrives

I WAITED patiently for many years for the spiritual veterinary surgeon to identify himself.

In 1966, I was sitting alone meditating one day when I became very aware of a young man. He gradually materialised in front of me. I was not afraid, but intrigued by his appearance.

I was, however, impressed by his round, smiling face and brown laughing eyes, which looked straight into mine. I noticed his skin was slightly dark. He was stockily built, not tall, of average height; he stood in a brilliant gold light that shimmered around him, making a sharp contrast to the turquoise blue clothing he wore from top to toe.

On his head he had a battered peak cap, which, I thought, had seen better days, a type of shirt garment without a collar, open at the neck with a shirt stud hanging loosely through the top buttonhole. His creased trousers and boots were as shabby as the rest of his attire.

"I wish to introduce myself to you in person," he said. I had to laugh at that and so did he. I knew what he meant. He carried on speaking:

"During my last life in your world, I was born into a Cockney family. Their name was Kemp. My parents gave me the name of Charles, but always called me Charlie and so did my mates. Although my old name belongs to a past chapter of my life, as we are now working closely together you may wish to refer to me as Charlie?" I agreed.

After I welcomed him and asked him why was he dressed like that, he smiled at me as one would with a little child, and replied, "I will explain to you later, but there are other things to talk about first with you."

Charlie moved closer to me and held out his hands. I put mine into his and felt great warmth and tremendous love coming from him.

After conveying his greetings and blessings from the

spirit world, he then continued by telling me: "In time the opportunity will come to you and another to open a healing centre for mankind. A second opportunity is also within its walls to open a healing sanctuary for sick animals, too. You will find in years to come that many of them will attend their sanctuary for healing. You will eventually lose count of the numbers. For the furtherance of our work together, the time is now right for us to meet face to face, so I am permitted to establish my identity to you." Charlie added:

"During your childhood and to the present day, in your many visits to my world while your physical body was sleeping, I have been your instructor, teacher and friend in the training of animal healing. I trust, dear colleague, you will still continue to work with me for the benefit of sick animals, as we have done side by side – always together – in the past.

"It will not be easy for you to declare to the public at large my existence, identity or my involvement in the field of healing animals in the flesh. But you, dear friend, possess the courage, determination and willpower to stand firmly in the face of all adversities, of which there will be many.

"Scorn and ridicule, without doubt, will be directed at you by those who cannot 'see.' The unbelievers will try in their fragile attempts to destroy your own convictions of my world.

"Many obstacles will be placed across your pathway. I cannot prevent others from using their own freewill or disperse their thoughts of mischievous intent if, and when, they so desire. But rest assured. No harm will come to you. And when any animal calls to you for healing, remember, I will always be there – by your side." As I listened to him, I knew there was no need for me to be fearful come what might.

No words can describe how I felt to see Charlie at long last, standing there. It was total confirmation of that which I already knew of life after physical death. After many years of just being aware of him, here he was, in fine form.

I was very excited, and delighted to have the pleasure of actually meeting and speaking to him. I started to thank him for coming to see me, but he kindly waved my assertions aside, saying: "There is no need to thank me, my friend, for like yourself I have donned the cloak of service to the Kingdoms of Life, especially that of the animals. You are not beholden to me, neither am I to you, as we are individuals. But we are as one and have a lot in common – the healing mission for animals."

Charlie spoke about the beneficial effects of healing for them. After a while I asked him if he had been a healer during his last earth life, how did he discover his healing gift, and how did it develop while he was here?

The following is Charlie Kemp's own account of the events that started him on his healing mission:

I was born in 1894 in London, at the Elephant and Castle. Like yours, my family was also very poor. My father, like yours, was hard working when work was obtainable, but we all loved one another. That was all that mattered. We managed to survive, even if at times we were very hungry. But I will not dwell on that because that situation is, for me, now past; it was one experience of life.

I always loved animals, regardless of their breed. I used to get frustrated, very upset, and felt so useless when I found a sick animal suffering and in pain. I prayed to God many times to help them out of their misery by letting them die for their keepers could not afford for them to have medical treatment of any sort. But nothing seemed to happen, and I had to continue to watch them suffer. But I still kept on praying!

Then one night, I was out walking when I came across a dear little mongrel lying in the gutter. He was crying in pain, and terribly injured. How or why I had no idea. Blood was pouring from his nose and mouth. I knew he was bleeding inside and through his stomach. His right back leg was broken; his ears were torn and bleeding; his left eye also. He did not seem to be long for this world. And he was crying so much I became very upset, worried, and angry that such a dear animal should be allowed to suffer like that.

I knelt down beside him and in despair called out to God and said out loud, "Lord, if you are there, Mate, for God's sake, help me to help this poor little creature." Suddenly, I saw a very bright light. It came over me and the little dog. He was, I could see, black and had a white spot over his right eye. I thought I was going barmy, for from nowhere there appeared lots and lots of pairs of hands with no arms attached to them. They were all around and above me and the dog – they even seemed to be coming up through the kerb stones and pavements: hands everywhere, some large, some small. I thought, "This is it Charlie, you won't be long now." I was scared out of my wits and could not move for fright!

I heard the church clock strike 8.00 pm. It was a winter's night, and quite clear. I glanced around to see if anybody else was seeing the hands like me, but the few people that were about just walked right past us, which made me think that perhaps I was going funny in the head. I remember that my physical body was fifteen years old at the time. Desperately I tried to gather my wits, when I heard a voice, a lady's voice. It was lovely, soft and gentle. I thought to myself, "This one is a proper lady," although I could not see her, which did not help me to steady myself! But the voice was still talking, telling me not to be afraid. By this time, I was terrified, barely able to speak and could not get any words out.

I looked down at the dog, thought he was dead, and that the Good Lord had after all at last heard my prayers for help and answered them.

Then I noticed two particular pairs of hands, one pair each side of me. They took hold of both of mine and placed them on the little dog, one on his stomach, the other on his poor broken little leg. It wasn't half funny because I could not see who the hands belonged to, but when they touched mine, I felt great heat passing through me onto the dog. There was also intense heat around us, which was coming from all the other many pairs of hands. Mind you it was nice, because they warmed me up as it was a cold night.

Although I could not see the invisible ones then, I said to them: "I will have to take my clothes off. You are making me feel extremely hot." It was daft really as I did not have a lot of clothes on. I could not afford many clothes anyway. Those I had were second-hand, not that it mattered.

The gentle voice informed me it would not be necessary as they would make me feel comfortable. The hands were all moving very gracefully and seemed to be intermingling, one with the other. Many colours, all different, were coming from them. I couldn't help but wonder what they were doing and come to that me as well. I felt rather silly, but also a wonderful sense of peace. My fear of them was easing away. As I looked up, I could at last see who the hands belonged to for there appeared a gathering of men and women complete with arms and legs.

Each one greeted me in love as though we had been friends for years. But they all seemed to be different from me because I could see through some of them. Others were in more solid form. I realised I was not afraid of them any longer. They made me feel I was a friend of theirs and wanted. It was a nice feeling.

The lady with the lovely voice stepped out from the rest, put her hands on my shoulders and told me to stand up, which I did. As I looked into her face, I saw that she was young and very beautiful. She had long, fair hair.

I noticed that the bright light which had been surrounding us all was gradually changing to a brilliant blue. It was moving, very active and swirling like a mist. I felt I was being wrapped up in a lovely warm blanket. Feeling quite safe, I put my hands into the blue light and felt a pleasant tingling sensation.

The fair haired lady told me to listen to her carefully. She said my prayers for help for the sick animals had been heard, and plans were made for me to be given the power of healing so that I could administer healing to them.

I hadn't got a clue of what she was talking about and said so. How could I of all people help sick animals to get better? She replied, "By laying your hands on them for you have the gift of healing." I said to her: "I have heard that Jesus Christ was a healer, but I'm no Jesus Christ. I still don't know what you are talking about. It does not make sense to me."

The lady took my hands in hers and said, "Just listen for a moment Charles." I said, "You can call me Charlie if you like." She laughed, said "All right," then went on to say that if and when I came across any of God's creatures which needed healing, and I put my hands on them, I would discover I would be able to help them to become better and relieve their suffering by the power of healing.

I'm sorry to say I was a bit rude to her at the time for I said: "I don't believe a word of what you are saying, and I don't understand it. Anyway, I would be the laughing stock with all of my mates. They would take the mickey out of me if I told them I could heal sick creatures just by touching them! They would think I've gone soft in the head!"

The lady simply said, "Come Charlie, I will show you," and put my hands on the little dog, again on his leg and stomach. He hadn't moved at all. She told me to be still and to think of him as being fit and well, which I thought was a bit daft as he had not moved at all and had stopped crying. I thought he was a goner.

But, Oh God, I again felt such great heat going into his little body. It flowed and pulsated through my fingers, a throbbing feeling. The light was still a beautiful blue, continually vibrating and moving around all of us, sending forth heat, which seemed to me as warm as standing in front of a big fire. But it was a different warmth: it was alive and overflowing with energy, which I later learnt was the healing energies. The colours were bright and glorious as I watched the blue gradually intermingle with them.

I thought at the time: "Why haven't we got a crowd of people to join us? Isn't anyone curious enough to come and see what is going on?" It all seemed so strange to me.

Anyway, I don't know how long I was kneeling and touching the little dog, but I thought I saw his tail move very slightly and looked up to tell the lady who, like all the others, was using her hands, moving them slowly over mine. I could not take my eyes away from her for the healing energies were pouring from her hands, and into and through mine.

I don't mind telling you I was very puzzled indeed. I asked her how was she doing it, and was it a form of magic? She told me I would learn the facts much later in life, how it was done, but not while I was on the earth plane, no, it certainly was not magic, and that everything I was witnessing was being carried out within the laws of the universe. She told me to continue touching the dog for a little while longer and wait and see what happened.

I had a feeling that the lady and the others watching were waiting for something to happen and said, "I'm not like Jesus Christ, ma'am, you know and raise things from the dead." She put her finger to her lips. I just carried on feeling a proper fool, with them all looking at me. Suddenly, the little dog started to wag his tail quickly. The bleeding from his nose, mouth, ears, eyes and stomach all stopped. I watched his wounds dry up, almost healed. He tried to pull himself up onto his legs. He had some difficulty owing to the leg which was still broken, but did not cry out in pain. I could see for myself he was, in fact, very much better.

The lady said to me: "There Charlie, do you need more proof of your healing power? Isn't this healing enough for you to decide for yourself whether or not you wish to administer healing to sick animals? The choice is yours. We have taken you through this healing lesson to show you what can be."

Well, I was flabbergasted and at the same time overjoyed to see the little dog making a comeback. I noticed the healing energies seemed to be cooling down just like a fire dying out. The heat from my hands was fading away as well. I was beginning to shiver with the winter cold. The beautiful colours slowly disappeared, leaving the brilliant blue in their place. In turn, the blue gave way to the bright white light that was originally the first to appear.

Meantime, I watched the people from the gathering merge into the light until I could no longer see them all. They certainly did not walk away, but seemed to glide so beautifully. Then the fair haired lady held my hands together. I remember how her lovely hair shone so as she stood in the light.

She said to me: "We all hope, Charlie, you will decide in the right direction. If so, I will be by your side." With a smile she bade me farewell, turned round and went into the light then disappeared taking the light with her. I stood still for a few seconds wondering if I had imagined it all. I could not believe what had happened.

I heard a train in the distance and assumed I had been away for a long time so glanced up at the church clock and thought my eyes were deceiving me for it was only five past eight o'clock. My experience, which I know now was a spiritual one, had only lasted for five minutes. I was astonished, for during that time such a lot had taken place. I looked around the street. It was deserted. I glanced down at the little dog who was tugging at my trouser leg to attract my attention. I picked him up in my arms. As I did so, I could have sworn he winked at me as I wrapped my old coat around him. I shall never forget how he nestled close to me when I told him I was going to take him to my home, and that we would be good friends, always together.

Secretly, I was hoping no one would turn up to claim him as theirs. I named him Spot because of the white patch over his eye. So I took him home, much to the annoyance of my dear old mum who bitterly complained that it would mean another mouth to feed. I had three brothers and three sisters younger than me. There was dad as well and now Spot, which made ten of us altogether, and times were hard so I could understand my mum being a bit put out!

All animals are psychic. My Spot knew he was not wanted. He was very upset so I told him he was going to stay just the same with us, even if my family at times did not have two half-pennies to rub together. My world, like yours, was different to the one of today. But I knew after what I had witnessed that somehow the Gathering of Friends would help me to find food for Spot. Little did I realise that he would be able to fend very well for himself in due course in a way that was going to bring the good name of my family into disrepute.

I had made a wooden splint for Spot's broken leg. This helped him to keep evenly balanced. I decided to take the opportunity of healing animals so placed my hands on Spot every day, hoping and praying for the best, for about fourteen days. I became more and more aware of the heat coming from my hands as I did so. I knew his leg was mending. It was getting stronger every day as he hopped about on three legs. But although I was able to get a few scraps of food for him, he was very thin. I was worried as I didn't want to lose him. We had a great love for one another and still have. He was indeed a comfort to me in my bleak physical young life. I knew he always understood every word I said to him.

The day came when I had to take the splint off Spot's leg. I was pleased to see it had healed very well. Spot was eager to show me his progress for he walked quickly around me. I then took him into our backyard. He was excited. We had developed a way of mental communication with each other. Suddenly he sat up in front of me, perfectly still and was saying to me, "I am going to run to show you how fit and well I am now." He did, and ran quite comfortably like a racehorse, without showing any sign of strain or a limp, or exhaustion. Then he stopped in his tracks, wagged his tail, looked up at me, smiled and was saying, "Thank you."

At that moment, my friend, I knew where my destiny lay. Laughed at or not, and maybe I would be called a looney by my mates and others as well, I was not going to be afraid of what people thought of me. I was going to tell them the Almighty had given me the power of healing His sick creatures.

Strange as it may seem at that moment of time, a sparrow fell down in front of Spot and me. It had a broken wing so I thought: "Here is another opportunity. I cannot overlook it. I must help this little bird." I took him indoors and cared for him. His wing mended so in due course he was able to fly away.

A short time later, I decided to venture out into the street with Spot to take him for a walk as he was keeping very well. I was still worried about him as he was not putting on any weight owing to his meagre diet. I was telling him I could not afford to buy him food to put some flesh on his bones. He glanced up at me and suddenly took off at great speed towards the shops, taking no notice of me when I called to him to come back. As he disappeared round the corner, I thought I had lost him forever.

But after a few minutes I saw him returning in the distance. He was walking awkwardly. I wondered what it was he appeared to be carrying. When he finally came up to me, I saw he had a large, heavy piece of fresh meat in his mouth. He dropped the meat on the ground. Well, we all have our faults and failings, haven't we? We all have to live, don't we? And it did solve my problem of feeding Spot and he was able to solve his too from time to time! Needless to say, he soon started to put on weight. He became a handsome-looking dog. Spot was about six years old when I found him. Even my old mum began to like him, and said he was paying for his bed and board whether by fair means or foul so was not unduly worried! I could understand her logic as my Spot was keeping us all well provided for and we were able to live like the gentry as when the need and demand arose, Spot was able at times to obtain the supplies. He would vary our menu and his own as well by bringing home sausages, bacon, faggots, saveloys, fish, fresh meat, bread and cakes. For good measure, on some of his mercy missions he would return with sweets and chocolate, which certainly did not come amiss to us!

Unfortunately, we all had to turn a blind eye on Spot's activities for we knew what it was like to feel the pangs of hunger – and he obviously believed in share and share alike, regardless whence the food came. Many times I was concerned and often tempted to ask him how he obtained it, but within myself I already knew the answer and thought of my mum's words, "Never look a gift horse in the mouth." But whenever dad and I did occasionally manage to get work, my beloved Spot was able to retire from his 'profession,' if only for a while.

In a way he became the breadwinner when we were in dire need. As you know, there were no handouts or easy pickings from the government of the day. The harsh rule was, "No work, no food!" So if it had not been for my dear Spot, my healing mission would not have got off the ground. I continued giving healing to sick animals, birds and other creatures that were sent to me. As time went on, the numbers increased. Many made good recoveries and were cured of their ailments.

My friend, the fair haired lady with the gentle voice, always came from the spirit world to link in attunement with me. I was her channel on earth for the administration of the healing energies to the animals. She also taught me how to develop further my healing gift. She was my dear teacher. I loved and respected her for the kindness she showed towards me.

Of course, Spot was always present during the healing sessions. He would be by my side to welcome the animals as they arrived, making them feel at home. He acted like a receptionist.

Then the time came for Spot to leave his body for good, to enter the spirit world. I was saddened, but accepted his going for he was old and had become very tired. I missed him a lot. Then my lady told me that Spot would be allowed to return to be with me from time to time, especially when animals were present for healing. So I eagerly waited for his spirit return. I did not have long to wait. One day as I held a sick cat, I heard my beloved Spot bark in greeting to me, and saw his spirit form.

It was my Spot without doubt: my lady had kept her word to me. I knew I would never lose him. When it was a healing day, he would arrive with her and take up his duties as before. The animals would see him and greet him warmly. I was thankful that their human keepers were not aware of him for they would not have understood. But there were several who had knowledge of the facts of life beyond the veil. They would inform me of Spot's presence. I used to give healing whenever I could. If I wasn't working I had more time. My dad gave me a corner in his hut in our backyard so I was able to take the dear animals, who always seemed to find their way to me, in there as my mum would never allow me to take them indoors. She said they would get in the way and under her feet, and that I and the animals would be out of sight and people would not be able to see what was going on. I felt sorry for her when she said that. After all, people do have eyes!

My dad was more interested, and sometimes stayed in the hut with me to watch. He was always pleased to see some of the animals were getting better. I used to like working in the hut for I could always feel the presence of the Almighty there.

When it comes to giving healing, it is not necessary for a healer to work in a palace or a mansion. The value of one's dwelling when on the earth plane is unimportant for God is everywhere, even in the humblest of abodes. In the world I now inhabit, grandeur is of no consequence whatsoever. It can never buy the riches of the Spirit. It belongs – for what it is worth – to the world of the material.

During my short life on the earth plane, I did not regret becoming a healer for it gave me fulfilment and a purpose in my life which made it all worth while, especially knowing that I had been granted the privilege of being an instrument of God's healing energies. With His blessings, many sick animals (not all, sadly) were cured of their ailments.

So my life continued until 1914 when the First World War broke out, the war which everyone unwisely thought would be the one to end all wars. If ever there was a figment of imagination, that was it. Nothing like looking at mankind through rose coloured glasses! I always had my doubts about peace reigning forever, like pigs might fly. On second thoughts, they might be able to in years to come taking into account the way scientists are secretly working behind closed doors.

Not being prone to violence, I had thought of becoming a conscientious objector, but knew within myself, I could not live like that. Although none of us really wanted to go into combat, me and my mates volunteered to fight for King and Country for we also valued our freedom. So to war we went, with thousands of other lads, like lambs to the slaughter. Into the first battle of the Somme we all charged, without sufficient training, weapons or supervision. I was twenty years old, old enough to witness man's inhumanity to man.

I remember just before I was blasted out of my physical body, I saw my dear Spot running quickly up to me on the battlefield, and wondered what he was doing there. I picked him up in my arms, when my body fell into pieces. Many people dressed in white suddenly appeared. Two women and a man glided up to us. The man said to me: "Have no fear, son. You will soon be home." The whole of the battlefield was lit up with a bright light. I noticed groups of men and women were helping those who also had left their shattered and crippled bodies.

I and the others (I still held Spot in my arms) were led away from the scene of battle into, and through, glorious colours. I heard such lovely music as I began to move upwards. I felt I was treading air. I could not feel solid ground beneath my feet. As I glanced downwards back at the earth plane, I saw it was covered in darkness, like a black mantle completely over it. The muffled sounds of guns firing and the anguished, terrible screams of men fighting were all left behind, as I and my spirit friends with the others entered into the beautiful spheres of the spirit world, where love, peace, harmony and light vibrate constantly, and where I now live.

On my arrival, I was overcome by complete surprise to be welcomed by many relatives, friends, and neighbours, all links with my old earth life. I was indeed very happy to return to my spiritual home, to feel so gloriously alive and to have my beloved Spot now always with me.

When it is time for you to open your healing sanctuary for animals, I will, of course, bring Spot with me, for him to greet them. He is looking forward very much to this mission.

I jokingly said to Charlie, "I hope Spot will not consider it a mercy mission whereby life saving food will materialise in the sanctuary." Charlie, having a great sense of humour, laughed a lot and saw the funny side of my remark. "No," he replied. "That was a material incident of necessity to survive in the physical body, long since forgotten by my Spot."

I asked Charlie if it would be possible for me to see Spot as I had not seen him at all. Neither had I been aware of him. "You will see him with me in your sanctuary at the right time, not before," he replied. "And I promise you will receive a portrait of him and one of myself as I was at the physical age of twenty years, the time of my arrival in the spirit world. You will always see me young as you see me now." I said to him, "When will I receive the portraits?" "Not until some years have passed," Charlie replied.

I had no idea then how they were to come my way, but knowing that the Spirit does not cross our T's and dot our I's for us, I could only wait and see. Here I will just mention that I had to wait twenty-one years before I received Charlie's portrait. It came through via my spirit artist, Anthony, on April 12, 1987. I am Anthony's channel for psychic art. This did not start to develop as a partnership with him until the year of 1967, but this is another story!

However, Charlie had kept his promise by enlisting the aid of Anthony, and gives an insight into the co-operation of the spirit people. Maybe, judging by our time standards, it took a long time, but this is of no consequence to the Spirit. And Spot's portrait? I received his via Anthony on September 14, 1988.

Charlie continued with the conversation and gave me further information about himself. He said:

"During my last earth journey, owing to my parents' very poor circumstances, they could not afford to send me to a veterinary college for training to become a veterinary doctor. I had no education. We did not even know then if those sort of colleges existed in those days, but, of course, I have since found out that they did, even if few and far between.

"So when I arrived in the world of the spirit to live, I was given the opportunity to study and develop further my healing gift for animals. I received expert tuition and worked with veterinary surgeons in the field of spiritual operational healing for animals on earth.

"It was not until I had studied well enough to meet the standard required of me by my teachers that I was allowed to choose an earth channel, such as yourself, to work with so together we could alleviate some of the suffering of the poor animals in the physical world. Our working partnership, dear friend, was planned a long, long time ago, ages before my last earth journey and before your present life. Now I look forward to the continuation of our healing work in Love."

At this stage of the conversation, I asked Charlie if his fair haired lady still worked with him in the field of healing? "No," he replied, "not now. She was the one who lit up my spiritual pathway for me and opened my eyes to my healing mission. My lady has moved on to help others on earth to see. Her work with me was only for a period of time, so to speak. I shall always be eternally grateful to her for helping me to open the door."

Charlie then said: "You are wondering why I come to you wearing tattered garments such as these? It is to give you a background – not that it is important – for it is now a past experience of my former earth life. I had to take any job I could find to help my parents to keep me. These replica clothes are ones I used to wear for my various jobs, including that of a coalman. I carried coal on my back more than once. To make a living, I was a rag and bone man for a short time.

"I wear this colour blue for as you know it is one of the main colours linked to the healing energies. I shall always come to you dressed like this so you will be able to recognise me at all times during the healing sessions." Charlie read my thoughts and added with a twinkle in his eyes, "No, I do not wear these particular clothes when we are not together for they are not necessary."

Charlie then said it was time for him to take his leave of me, and that he would return by materialising again.

He did so a month later when I was alone and sitting quietly in meditation. He was wearing the same turquoise blue garments as before. Smiling at me, he held my hands in greeting. I remember how warm his hands were. As I looked at his face, I thought what a lovable character and engaging personality he was – and will always be!

Charlie again spoke of the many benefits animals received by spiritual healing. In his view, they are far more receptive to healing energies than some humans. I agreed. As Charlie stated, "Animals have no mental blocks whatsoever and come to that no prejudice either, for in their love and complete trust they are open receivers." He added:

"We are working together in the pioneering field of spiritual operational healing for animals. Although you will be entranced while working with me, you will not be using any surgical tools of any description for they are not necessary. No animal under our care will be harmed or distressed in any way.

"I know you will always bear in mind our healing mission for them. It is – and always will – be vitally important for they are a very deserving cause and will be even more in need at the callous hands of man as they continue to be fodder for his vile, cruel experiments upon them. Already obnoxious acts of cruelty and unspeakable violence to our beloved, furred, winged, feathered and other friends have been instigated by scientists, in the name of science and medicine – or so they say. These inhuman souls are working secretly behind locked doors, hiding their faces.

"My colleagues, myself and your spirit self have, at times, travelled to the evil places of torture on your earth plane, where the poor creatures can only scream in agony and appalling suffering under the hands of their torturers, male and female alike, who are not capable of love, compassion, mercy or pity for their hapless and helpless innocent victims."

At this stage of the conversation I asked Charlie why did he not release the animals from their physical bodies and suffering when we were witnessing the cruelties being carried out? He replied:

Like others, whether it be my side of the curtain or yours, I am not a law unto myself. Therefore, like others, I must abide by the natural laws of the universe. There is always the law of cause and effect. All living creatures on earth, including man, have a life span, which should be lived naturally from start to finish as planned.

But when animals and other species of life are deliberately murdered under scientific "experiments," I, with my healing team, and many other healing teams working elsewhere, are very often present to help and comfort the dying animals so they do not enter our world of light in terror and fear. We help them to adjust to their new spiritual environment and look after them.

Languishing in the torture chambers are hundreds of animals, bound and tied, unable to move, some only able to cry out softly in their torment, not yet suffering a violent physical death, but undergoing intolerable pain through indescribable injuries so cold bloodedly inflicted upon them. At least we are able to alleviate for a time, to a lesser degree, some of their suffering by administering healing to them. Unfortunately, our efforts in trying to restore unity, balance and harmony within the poor twisted, pain racked little bodies, that were once beautiful and near perfect, is only short lived.

For the violent abusers soon return to their grim, unnatural, evil tasks and set about destroying – unbeknown to them, in their complete ignorance of spiritual matters – the good, beneficial healing we have carried out, and – terrifyingly – the poor animals as well.

We are constantly on guard to protect them as much as possible from the evil for while man on earth acts towards his fellow creatures without love and mercy – as he does and he intends to continue – we cannot stop him, as you are aware. He is at liberty to use his own free will at all times. Therefore, he is entirely responsible for his dreadful deeds. His long list of inhuman crimes against all kingdoms is endless.

While he was talking to me, Charlie appeared to be deeply moved in his compassion for his beloved animals and at the same time expressed strongly his great concern of the limited life span on earth of all creatures at the hands of mankind. He spoke with sincerity. I became very aware of the great depth of feeling within him, and at the same time realised that I was indeed very fortunate to call him my friend and teacher. His clothing had turned into a much deeper shade of turquoise blue. He had materialised to such an extent that he could easily have been mistaken as being in a physical body, but I knew he wasn't. The gold light moving around and over him became more brilliant than ever.

Charlie picked up the threads of the conversation where he had left off before, and said to me:

I feel such deep sadness, as do those in my world who work towards the welfare and happiness of animals, to be the bearer of unpleasant information in the extreme, to have to tell you that in time to come there will be many working under the guise of scientists living on your plane whereby according to their man-made blue prints, they will be able to "create" new animals.

By the time of your earth, in the years of the late 1990s there will be animals of different designs, poor monstrous creatures on the production lines of life. At present none of them is known to man. But he will learn a hard and surprising lesson, for they in their turn will bite the hands that create them. And where lucre talks, the unscrupulous "creators" will not hesitate in the selling of their wares on demand.

They will discover the price they will have to pay for their misguided intellects and egoes. Their horrific works of black creations will be beyond measure. So be it. All the designers have chosen their own pathways. I and my colleagues cannot prevent them.

Charlie then continued by informing me that it was not only the animal kingdom that was to be recreated by man, but also all the living creatures of the world. Insect and plant kingdoms will not be excluded. Neither will the feathered kingdoms for birds manufactured by their creators will make the dinosaurs of centuries past look like midgets. Man, by his folly, will reverse into ages past and walk backwards instead of forwards, as time will tell.

I was forty-five years old when Charlie called on me for the second time, and must admit I could not really accept all of the mentioned information he gave me then. But now I accept it, word for word, in this day and age!

We had a very long conversation by thought power. Charlie continued to tell me that scientists, not knowing when to stop, would be experimenting with human and animal organs for later use in other bodies which did not contain them in the first place, and that mankind will also be "designer created" to great stature, width and height, to enable him to control the monsters that will be at large in our material world.

I remember asking Charlie if he could tell me when all these dreadful changes would take place. He replied, "Dinosaur man and dinosaur monsters will be on the earth by the twenty-third century." When I asked why did he refer to the word "dinosaur," Charlie said, "So that you will have a guideline of the size of those to come – eventually."

All through the years I have often thought of Charlie's words to me. I knew one day I would put pen to paper when the time was right, as it is now.

Through the years I have not seen Charlie in the materialised form again as I did in 1966. As previously stated, it is not necessary now. But I have seen him clairvoyantly hundreds of times since to the present day. And his dear Spot? I was not even aware of him until our Pet's Corner Healing Sanctuary was opened in 1972. Then I saw him for the first time with Charlie. When he arrives, Spot is always by his side to welcome animals when they attend for healing.

I will just add that my husband and I have countless times witnessed the remarkable healing of many seriously ill animals who had been given up by their own vets as incurable. Indeed, some had swallowed poison. But under the care of Charlie, and by his knowledge and skill, they have fully recovered, being restored to good health.

So I will now leave readers to examine the recorded cases in this book so they can find out for themselves the quality and depth of Charlie Kemp's wonderfully advanced spiritual healing work.

First, I should like to bring to the readers' attention the following rules:
- According to the Veterinary Surgeons' Act (1966) all animals attending our centre must already be under the care of their vets.
- We do not under any circumstances issue prescriptions to their owners for animals.
- We do not administer drugs in tablet form or otherwise to animals.

- We do not interfere with drugs or treatments already being given or advised by the animals' own vets.
- We do not request at any time that owners should refrain from taking animals to their vets.
- We do not advise against surgery if it has been suggested by members of the veterinary profession. Decisions taken are the animal owner's responsibility entirely, not ours.
- We do not "manipulate" animals in any way.
- At no time do we advise any animal to be "put down" if suggested by their vets. Again, it is the owners who must decide for themselves.
- We never give owners false hope by promising cures or improvements for their pets.
- We do not charge fees – donations are accepted – for our healing services for animals or humans, whether it be by contact healing (the laying-on of hands) or absent healing.
- Animals which are brought to us come as a last resort after failing to respond to professional treatments.

With the above I will include the following, a happy follow-up to an incident that took place in 1984 due, no doubt, to an anonymous letter writer.

At the time I was writing short articles for the "Dorking and Reigate Times" newspaper.

One day, my husband and I were very surprised – and a little apprehensive to say the least – to receive a letter dated January 9, 1984, from the Royal College of Veterinary Surgeons. It stated:

Dear Sirs, The Royal College's attention has been drawn to the terms of an advertisement for the centre which appeared recently in an edition of the "Dorking and Reigate Times," stating, "Healing for all complaints and animals."

We would be interested to learn the nature of the healing you carry out in relation to animals bearing in mind the provision of the Veterinary Surgeons Act (1966). We look forward to hearing from you, (etc).

We had no idea whatsoever that by placing the advertisement in the paper we were acting against the Veterinary Surgeons Act. In fact, we did not know such an act existed.

One morning I was washing up at the kitchen sink when

my beloved Charlie Kemp suddenly appeared and stood beside me. I must admit I was not thinking of him at that moment of time, although I had on a receiving the letter previously sent out my thoughts to him for help and guidance. He placed his hand on my shoulder and said to me:

"I am aware of your anxiety regarding our animal healing and the outcome concerning the letter. The matter in question needed to be brought out into the open to be discussed from all sides, including ours! Have no fear or worries. In two years hence of your time you will find that the pendulum will swing in your favour and for all other animal healers, too. All complications that have arisen are man-made and will be resolved. You and others will be given the go-ahead, a clear pathway, even to advertising your healing services for animals. Do not forget – two years from now."

I thanked him. Charlie, after patting me comfortingly on my shoulder, slowly disappeared from view. On January 23, 1984, we received a very nice letter from the Royal College of Veterinary Surgeons as follows:

Dear Mr and Mrs Sowter, We are most grateful to you for responding to our enquiry of January 9 in such helpful terms. We have noted that, after appropriate consultation with the National Federation of Spiritual Healers, reference in advertisements to animal healing has been withdrawn, etc.

So the waiting time continued. Gerald and I quietly carried on with animal healing, but not advertising the fact, for the next two years.

Finally, the great day arrived when in March, 1986, "Psychic News" published the good news. We were overjoyed and delighted to read the article by Tony Ortzen, the then Editor. I will only include parts of it. It was headlined, "Royal College gives green light to animal healing." The story stated: "In a milestone-marking move, it had been announced that spirit healers can minister to sick and suffering animals . . . and stay within the law. Furthermore, the Royal College of Veterinary Surgeons even commissioned a Queen's Counsel to clarify the situation, so after a long period of doubt, the situation has been clarified. Absent healing has also been given the green light.

"Trouble first brewed for one husband-and-wife team, Irene and Gerald Sowter. Difficulties emerged after they offered healing in a local paper."

"Psychic News' " advertising manager commented: "It is good news that the Royal College of Veterinary Surgeons and healing organisations reached agreement about treatment for animals. With the threat of persecution removed, PN can now accept announcements offering healing to all living creatures."

Needless to say, while reading such glad tidings, we gave a great sigh of relief and felt sure our healing colleagues here and in the world of the spirit did the same.

I have often wondered since if the person, whoever it was, who in 1984 drew the Royal College of Veterinary Surgeons attention to our activities in the first place, realised the good deed that was carried out for us - eventually! Charlie Kemp said to me when Gerald and I were sitting quietly in meditation: "Spare a kind thought or two for the person who started the ball rolling for us. We never waste an opportunity when it is provided."

So I will take this opportunity to thank the anonymous one, not forgetting, of course, to say "Thank you" to Charlie for the part he played in bringing about the happy ending (behind the scenes) as he had promised.

Chapter 3

Spiritual Operational Contact Healing

DUKE OWEN had been a beautiful golden retriever, but when his owners brought him to us he was a very sorry sight. His stomach was grotesquely swollen. He could hardly stand. His lovely brown eyes were dim and watery.

Duke's worried owners, Roy and Annette Owen of Bracknell, had been informed by his vet that he had a serious liver malfunction. He wanted them to take Duke to Bristol University for further investigation as orthodox treatment had failed to improve his condition. As a last resort, Mr and Mrs Owen decided there and then to bring him to our centre. Poor Duke, with his huge stomach, which to him must have felt like weighing a ton, did not seem to care whether he lived or died. As Gerald and I placed our hands upon him, I felt a sudden electric shock go into Duke's body. Then I became aware of Charlie standing beside us. His beloved Spot was sitting by the side of Duke on the table. He was talking to him. They had an instant rapport, which caused Duke to relax and become more at ease. Charlie asked me if I was ready to commence healing with him for Duke. I agreed.

The following is an exact account of our records of Duke's remarkable cure from start to finish, written by Annette and Roy Owen:

Duke captured our hearts when he came into our home at twelve weeks old. He had all his injections and progressed to normal puppyhood. Then about September/October of 1986 when he was eleven months old, he started to drink a lot, and to go off his food. He began to lose weight. His water consumption went up until he was drinking twelve pints a day. We thought Duke was diabetic and took him to the vet. The vet put him on a course of diuretics, then blood tests and antibiotics. Duke got steadily worse.

We contacted Irene and Gerald Sowter, and had Duke put on their absent healing list. By early December 1986, Duke's stomach had started to swell. After more blood tests, the vet told us Duke had a liver malfunction. Although the vet didn't actually say it, we knew Duke had a growth. He could no longer stand or walk, and had to be carried. The vet could do no more for him, and wanted us to take him to Bristol University. He explained that Duke would be there for a week. Tests would be made to determine where in the liver the disorder was. If not too deep, they would operate.

We decided to think it over and let the vet know the next morning. After a lot of heart searching we decided to keep Duke at home. He wasn't in any pain, but had been through enough. We knew that if he went to Bristol that would be the end. So we told the vet of our decision. He said he would put Duke down if that's what we wanted. He was told that wasn't the case: we would give Duke lots of loving care, and when the time came would do the necessary.

An appointment was made for Duke to go to see Irene and Gerald on December 11, 1986 for contact healing. Duke was carried into the sanctuary. Charlie Kemp, the spirit vet, operated on him. No incision was made with a knife as Charlie used Irene's hands. At no time was Duke in any pain or discomfort. No promises of a recovery were made, just promises of healing help. There was no pain. An appointment was arranged for the next week.

During that week Duke progressed. He started walking, eating chicken casserole, and putting on weight. By Christmas 1986 he was his old self, the best Christmas present our family could have wished for. All during this time he was receiving contact healing every week.

Unfortunately, Duke had a relapse in January 1987. His stomach started to swell again. He was being sick. Even so, he still maintained his energy. Because of bad weather we were unable to go for contact healing. Duke's stomach got bigger. The rest of his body lost weight.

When we were able to attend for healing again, Charlie Kemp gave Duke his second operation in February 1987.

Still Duke got bigger in the stomach and looked as if he was going to burst. At no time did he go back to the vet. Then Duke brought up some black matter, just small pieces in his vomit. Every week he attended for healing. After this last bout of sickness, the swelling reduced a little.

Charlie operated again – for the third time – and told us to watch and see if Duke brought up or passed anything in his urine or motion. A few days later, Duke brought up his growth. It was about the size of a tennis ball and looked like black peat with fibres running through it. There was hardly any smell.

After this Duke really progressed. There was no swelling. His urine and motion were normal. Duke had an extra abundance of energy. He started to gain weight and to eat quite normally. He is still attending for healing, although this is now being reduced to once a fortnight, and then once a month, if progress is being maintained. Thanks to Charlie Kemp, Irene and Gerald, we have a normal seventeen-month-old Duke that we would not have had if he had gone to Bristol.

This was signed April 1987. Duke came bouncing into the centre in May and June, and was maintaining excellent progress. His last visit was in August 1987. Charlie, with Spot by his side, stated, "There is no need for Duke to return for contact healing as he is in such good health." So he discharged him. I watched Spot as he also bid him farewell. Talking afterwards to Charlie, I asked him if Duke had gone to Bristol University would the vets there have been able to save him. He replied: "Sadly no, owing to the advanced state of the growth. They would only have carried out an exploratory operation on him." Charlie then added that by acting on their "instincts," the Owens had provided him with the opportunity of trying to help their beloved pet.

We received a Christmas card in 1988 from the Owen family and Duke, along with a letter. Part of it read: "Duke sends you his love and a big hug, but I'm afraid no kisses as he never kisses anyone. He is keeping well."

We often think of him with great fondness. But for the grace of God, he almost went through the spirit door. We received Christmas cards from the Owen family and Duke in 1989, 1990 and 1991. At the time of writing in 1992, he is still very well indeed.

Bandit Eggars

WHAT a sorry state poor little Bandit was in when we had the privilege of meeting him in June 1986. He was certainly a gentleman of pleasure – having enjoyed sexual delights with his lady friends – so one could quite understand his frustration when his vital organs ceased to work.

Roy Eggars, of Bexhill-on-Sea, explained by his letter: "Our mongrel dog, Bandit, who was then fifteen years old, was suddenly taken seriously ill. We thought he would not survive the night. The following morning we took him to the vet, who said Bandit had an infection allied to a growth in the testicles. He prescribed some tablets and gave him an injection.

"We made a return visit two days later, but there was no improvement to report. The vet suggested that if the treatment was not effective, an operation might be tried, but was reluctant to pursue this course in view of Bandit's age and heart condition, which showed signs of deterioration. A change in tablets was prescribed. For the next four days we wavered between slight improvement and deciding whether to have Bandit put down to prevent further suffering, as he was in a very poor condition, not eating and hardly able to walk.

"We decided to ring Mr and Mrs Sowter's healing centre. They kindly gave us an immediate appointment. On examination, Charlie Kemp diagnosed a growth in Bandit's testicles and said although an operation had been suggested, it would make the growth spread. He promised that his treatment would reduce the growth and stop Bandit enduring further suffering. This proved to be true.

"The swelling and hardness in his testicles disappeared during further visits in the ensuing weeks. Bandit's general state of health improved, becoming better than it had been prior to his illness!

"As proof of this fact, we had two visits from the local police a couple of months later. They called as a result of complaints by people in the next road that Bandit was pursuing their bitch and fighting other dogs. Fourteen months later, he is still enjoying life without any recurrence of the trouble."

Regarding Bandit's first visit to us, Charlie operated on his testicles and penis. After two further healing sessions, not "operations," whereas the cancer had previously been large and hard, there was no sign of it at all. Bandit was eating very well, and regained his energy so Charlie discharged him, much to his delight.

Thinking of him brings to my mind the old saying, "There's plenty of life in the old dog yet." So it was with him. Bandit continued with his hot life style and many conquests until it was time to depart this life at the age of seventeen years. I hope Bandit was not too disappointed to discover when he arrived on the Other Side that the physical pleasures do not apply to the spirit . . . but at least he died happy!

Slippers Parris

A LETTER came from Mrs. Parris of Sussex in August 1986. "Please could my little miniature Dachshund, Slippers, have absent healing?" it asked. "He is suffering with his back. The vet has given him tablets, but I would like him to have your help too."

Charlie stated he had seen Slippers, and the poor little fellow was suffering from a slipped disc, a weakness with Dachshunds. He could not walk, and was very uncomfortable indeed as his back hurt him. Slippers would receive operational absent healing.

Gerald and I linked in thought with Charlie for it to commence. I watched as Charlie's hand worked quickly over Slipper's spine without any manipulation.

Three weeks afterwards came good news when we received the following from Mrs. Parris: "It is really amazing. My little dog is much better already. The vet told me to treat him like an invalid and not to let him run up and down stairs or jump on beds, etc. He also told me to keep the pain-killing tablets which he gave me to put in the cupboard in case they were needed. My thanks to Charlie. We have not needed them!"

Charlie thought the idea of treating Slippers like an invalid and not to let him move was most unwise. He said:

"By all means pamper him, if he is not showing any signs of recovery. But as he is making good progress, he needs to be given every encouragement to lead his life normally.

"Animals are psychic and very aware indeed of negative or positive thoughts towards them from those who love them. If Mrs. Parris had thought negatively regarding his condition (fortunately she did not) Slippers would soon react to her thoughts and begin to act like an invalid. Animals, just like some humans, love to be fussed over and coddled."

In September came another letter from Mrs. Parris, saying: "Slippers continues to make good progress. He is really a happy little dog, and loves to run around and go for walks. My daughter had a sitting last week with medium Anthony Giles at Seaford. He said to her, 'You have a little dog that had back trouble.' 'Yes,' said my daughter. 'He is my mothers.' 'Tell her,' said Mr. Giles, 'that his back will be all right now.' Tell me, Irene. Would this be Charlie speaking? I felt it must be."

It was indeed! Knowing Charlie, he would not waste an opportunity to send a message through to Mrs. Parris to reassure her that Slippers would be all right. Mr. Giles picked up the message accurately for Mrs. Parris has informed me that Slippers "is running around like a two year old puppy, with no trouble at all with his back." We have a photograph of him and he is delightful.

Rita Matterini

POOR little Rita, a very beautiful black and white cat, was not very old when she was carried into the centre. As I looked at her I thought she would not be here for much longer.

Rita was constantly vomiting, not eating at all, and had lost an awful lot of weight. Even Spot looked more concerned than usual! Miss Matterini said the vet "has done all he can for her, but cannot help further." Charlie agreed, and stated he would do his best. But aside to me, he was doubtful at that moment of time whether or not he would be able to help Rita to survive on the earth plane as her condition was extremely serious owing to Feline Dysantonomia.

As I set to work in trance with Charlie and Gerald, I became very aware of the discomfort within Rita's little body, especially in her abdomen where Charlie said it was necessary to operate. No wonder Rita was so ill! But she began to purr a little as she relaxed under our hands, and knew we were all there to help her.

The operation did not take long, about ten minutes. When Charlie finished, he asked me to inform Miss Matterini that he was not promising a miracle cure, or even an improvement with her little pet, but just to wait for results.

Rita attended the centre twice, the second time for a check-up, when only fourteen days had elapsed since her spirit operation. I was more than thankful to see how remarkably she had recovered.

Miss Matterini, full of smiles, and very relieved, said: "Look at Rita! She seemed to recover soon after the healing. I don't know what happened as I do not understand healing, but something must have taken place for Rita was so very ill, and I was worried she would have to be put down. Now she has stopped vomiting completely, and is eating normally. She has also put on weight as you can see." I did not tell her how close to passing Rita had been – there was no need – but as I looked at her, her glowing good health and lovely, shining bright eyes, I thought, "Whatever would we do without our beloved Charlie, and his faithful companion Spot?" Rita is still strong and healthy – and has never looked back, not once.

Harvey Delaney

PHEW! What a life force, Harvey, a handsome black standard poodle, had within him. As he bounded into the centre I thought, "This dog is going to live forever!"

When I touched him, I heard Charlie say: "Gently stroke Harvey's head. He is hyperactive through eating 'doctored' tinned foods. As children and adults are becoming allergic to foods tainted by unnecessary dangerous chemicals, so poor animals are made to suffer in similar vein, as you are well aware. The substances with which Harvey is being fed stimulate his mobility and activities, which I am sure must exhaust his loving caring owners, the Delaneys.

"Nevertheless, I find Harvey a very healthy dog. If he were a human, to use a popular expression in your world he would be termed a workaholic. I will try to slow him and calm him down a little."

According to Jean Delaney, Harvey liked to "pull things about" in her home, which I believe was putting it mildly! After four sessions of contact healing, Charlie discharged him, for Harvey was taking life more sedately. Perhaps he realised there is no point in trying to beat the clock?

Nicky Stanton

WE always receive a lot of mail from people of all walks of life requesting absent healing. Some are negative by thought, or in great despair, others more hopeful. But there are always those who despite their overbearing trials and tribulations, can see the funny side and write letters to create laughter, a wonderful gift to possess! Ralph Stanton, Nicky's owner, is such a person for amidst all the suffering we witness with animals and humans alike, reading his letters from time to time, has given us many a laugh, which has made our day, thanks to his sense of humour.

"Nicky has got over the flu, but has been up watering of a night," said Mr Stanton. "He has some water problems spotted with blood. I realise now how he got his name for he's a dirty little devil. If not watched, like me will not go out." I'm treating him to a course of 'Tibs' as a tonic and may have some myself if they do any good . . ."

When we received this letter, Charlie stated Nicky had a cancer in the bladder, was not at all well and needed help, which he would endeavour to give via absent operational healing.

Ten days later another letter arrived from Mr Stanton, who lived in Dorset: "Nicky had us in a panic after he came in swollen like a balloon on Saturday evening, unable to pass water. I placed him in a box with newspaper for he was almost in a coma, and asked for spirit help. I put my hands on him, doubting he would last the night.

"On Sunday morning, he was sitting up in the box, which was soaking wet and bloodstained. Through Sunday and Monday he was passing a lot of blood and water, and finally pus matter.

"I did not think he would stand a trip to the vets, or last, at that rate. He was not in pain. On the Tuesday morning he stood up purring as if to say 'I'm all right.' The bleeding lessened. By Wednesday night he was scratching to go out all night, but it was too cold in his condition.

"He has continued to progress. His bladder seems to be working normally, so much so that I had newspaper down everywhere and burned incense to counteract the aroma. This morning he's out running around his patch. So our grateful thanks to all for what to us appeared to be a miracle." Two months afterwards a third progress report stated: "Nicky is back to health, and eating well. His bladder is fine now."

Charlie mentioned to me that he was not a worker of "miracles" as they did not exist; it was just a matter of "good happenings" taking place, when and wherever it was possible. These are always within the laws of the universe. But do not forget, we also have our failures.

He had found Nicky a good patient, one willing to co-operate. Charlie was pleased to see Nicky's owner did not, after all, decide to take a course of "Tibs." However, he did appreciate his brand of humour!

Chapter 4

Training Behind the Scenes

ALTHOUGH I have been a healer of the human race for many years, as well as a clairvoyant and clairaudient medium, when I was about twenty-five years old I was surprised to be informed quite suddenly and unexpectedly by learned ones in the world of spirit that further development of my ability to heal animals would commence shortly and at the right time. Not only would I have a healing sanctuary for people, but also one for animals in the same building. How accurate my spirit friends were with their information, even if it was all to take place years ahead. For that is precisely what occurred in 1972.

Actually, I had never thought for one moment of this happening. But the spirit proposal then jolted my memory back to the events I had experienced during my early childhood days and teenage years, which I shall recount shortly. I then realised that I was being brought to a greater understanding as to why these had taken place, and the full meaning of them.

However, I did think that as the Spirit had taken the trouble to approach me at that moment of time, there would be a sound reason and purpose behind their proposal as I have always found after years of experience working with the dear spirit friends – and still do.

But I also knew that, as with all things, whether in due course I accepted or rejected the plan offered to me, responsibility for deciding either way was entirely mine. I instinctively knew it would not be necessary to seek advice elsewhere, but to wait until the time of the Spirit was right for me to commence the work in earnest.

During the whole of my life, I have had many lovely and outstanding experiences in other fields of my spiritual work. Regarding the above, I can remember when going to sleep as a very small child, at different times my spirit self would travel through the curtain to the world beyond.

On occasions, animals of various kinds were present. I sensed my visits were for a purpose, but owing to my tender years, did not then understand to what extent. However, my exciting visits to the Other Side were of far greater importance than I had ever realised at the times they took place. Gradually, it dawned on me that I was receiving training, guidance and instruction behind the scenes from the dear learned ones in the spirit world regarding animal healing.

Sometimes there was one particular soul, who seemed to draw close to me. I instinctively knew he was of Cockney origin, but was never able to see his face, only a glimpse occasionally of a misty shadowy figure. I always felt comforted and uplifted by his presence – as I do today – just knowing he was there beside me, helping and advising when I was giving healing to animals. But it was not until much later in my life that I found out actually who he was.

I became aware of him, talking to me and teaching me, a dim memory of trying to answer his questions. There was a feeling of being pleased when I replied correctly, and not too happy when my answers were not the right ones. Oh yes, I certainly had to learn my lessons. It appeared that if not attending a university on the Other Side, I was definitely going back to school. It was very frustrating and extremely aggravating when I awoke and could not always recall what the questions were about. It was not until a much later stage of my life that the spiritual plans with this gentleman were to unfold before me, and the major role he was going to play in my development in the field of animal healing.

I asked to be given his name many times, but without success. I knew I would receive it at the right time, and not before. When I awoke in the mornings I could not always remember what had taken place. Recollection was often hazy, other times more clear. During my conscious state, regardless of what I happened to be doing at the time, whether at school and later at work, or carrying out menial tasks of domesticity, suddenly I would have a flash, a revelation, but only for a moment or two. It was rather like a jig-saw puzzle, fitting in a piece to complete the picture or just like standing outside a window looking in. This helped me to grasp what had been happening.

I dare say there will be those who will ponder on the inevitable question as to why do we not remember everything that takes place while our physical bodies are resting in sleep.

Without going into a lengthy description of how the spirit functions at this stage – and no-one knows all the answers – I feel that the answer to the question is that we are not meant to remember everything. If we did so, we would become like robots. We must always operate our own free will, think for ourselves in all things and find our own individual pathways, spiritually and materially, whether we wish to or not. All through my life I have preferred to find mine. Admittedly, like so many others, it has not been easy!

During the sleep state, I remember walking into the breathtaking beauty of the brilliant rays of colours of so many different hues, throbbing with great energy, giving out the life force that abounds in the spirit world. Their warmth is tremendously uplifting. A wonderful sense of untold depths of peace exists. Harmony and love reign everywhere.

I had a beautiful feeling of floating as light as a feather, and being enveloped in the welcoming rays of light, moving with them as they rotated over and all around me. One cannot describe the sheer ecstasy of dancing when listening to the glorious music and singing in the realms of the spirit. I could have stayed there forever, not wanting to return to the conscious state!

Often there were quite a lot of children of all ages with me. We would be met by our spiritual teachers and taken to our various "classrooms" where we could study and learn the many aspects of psychic and spiritual phenomena to prepare us for our future work as healers, clairvoyants, clairaudients and the rest during this span of our earth lives.

Many a time while attending and trying to concentrate on lessons in my school of the material world, I very much wished I was sitting in one of the spirit world. There is no comparison between the two. I was often rapped over the knuckles with a ruler by teachers in the physical body for not paying enough attention!

Little did they know that two of my little classmates,

Elsie and Timothy (who I write about later) travelled with me many times for instruction, and to learn the art of animal healing in the spirit world.

As previously mentioned, several animals of different kinds were present. In the spirit classrooms they would be gathered together in little groups. On some occasions I could remember, our spiritual instructors would demonstrate to us how to place our hands on the little "patients" who, of course, being in the spirit world were very healthy indeed. They all loved practising as much as we did. It was indeed great fun. I have never known such school lessons to be so enjoyable.

What I do remember during these healing sessions is that if any of the spiritual teachers spoke of colours, they just seemed to appear. They were naturally exercising their thought power. Different colours were pointed out to us as having great potential healing properties for certain ailments within the physical body of humans, animals and all other living forms of life.

When our healing lessons were over, we were then allowed to take our animal "patients" for walks. In fact, it often seemed they were taking us! For they led us to the most delightful places in the spirit world and introduced us to many other animals who appeared to be their friends. We would stay and talk with them all for a while before we were sent back to earth to awake to the conscious state. More than once, all the children were grouped together by one of the teachers and counted before we bade farewell until the next time.

I shall never forget that on one spiritual visit which I was allowed to remember from start to finish, we were taken into a large hall. The walls were vibrating with silver and gold intermingling, but there did not appear to be a floor to stand on. Although we had no difficulty in standing and keeping our balance as we moved around, below us there was a moving substance, which was very beautiful, like Mother of Pearl. It reminded me of a pale rainbow. Above us was the same that seemed to go on to great heights forever.

There were several male and female teachers present whom we had not met before. I have not seen them since to the present day. Some wore robes of gold, others robes of silver, and the rest garments of Mother of Pearl.

All these spiritual beings shone with such brightness of light and radiance that it would have been impossible to have looked upon them whilst being in the physical body. I noticed that slowly their robes shed forth rays of gold, silver and Mother of Pearl. They all intermingled, one with the other. The hall generated a heat which was not uncomfortable or unbearable. I was fascinated by the wondrous sight and extremely aware of the love and harmony that prevailed everywhere.

Then a procession of assorted animals entered the hall. I watched as they formed a circle. There were many known to man, including some from wild life. I particularly loved the white polar bear which was exuding friendship to all and sundry. There were two lions, a tiger, several varieties of monkeys and other species of jungle life apart from domestic animals. Surprising as it may seem, peace reigned. Neither I nor the other children with me were afraid. We all felt quite at ease.

Then the teachers took each one of us by the hand and led us to stand individually in front of and facing an animal. I was hoping to be in front of the polar bear, but it was not to be for I was placed in front of a large dog, a golden retriever. He was gorgeous! He smiled at me in greeting, and lifted up his front paw to me, which I held for a few moments.

The teacher dressed in gold, standing with me, spoke to me by thought power and told me to hold out my hands to my patient." I noticed that the other children with their teachers behind them were all doing the same to theirs.

As I looked at my hands, the colour gold, with great heat, emerged from them and vibrated towards the dog, who was joyfully waiting with his eyes shut to receive it. There he stood perfectly still. So were all the other animals.

I watched my patient slowly being covered from head to toe in the gold healing energy which was still coming from my hands. As I glanced around at the others, some of the children were also giving forth the gold healing energy to their patients. Some were using silver energy and others the Mother of Pearl. The animals were being covered by these individual colours.

Our teachers then instructed us to close our eyes so we

could feel these living life-saving forces within us. For a few seconds I found this so exhilarating that I was lifted off my feet. I am sure all the other pupils must have felt the same.

I noticed the teachers dressed in gold only produced gold energy, those in silver, silver energy and the others attired in Mother of Pearl, Mother of Pearl energy. Thinking back, they must have all been specialists in their own particular healing fields.

As there is no time in the spirit world – how lovely it is not to have to watch a clock! – I cannot say how long we were in the beautiful hall. Like all good things, our visit had to come to an end, but not before I watched the healing energy slowly disappearing completely from my hands and into the dog. The same was happening to the other children and their animals until there was not a trace of energy visible. The heat had also gone from my hands.

We were all standing, including our "patients," in the same place when at a given signal – a lifting of the hand by a teacher who was apparently the leader of the group – the animals then burst into song . . . without words! They were definitely singing, in perfect harmony and could have taught some of our modern pop groups a lesson or two! There was not – to my untrained ear – a flat note coming from any of the spirit animals. It was an extraordinary finale to a most pleasurable spiritual visit.

We stood and waited for the singers to be led away, again in a procession. They used their thought power towards us all, saying "au revoir." A delightful moment indeed!

Although the rays from the teachers' robes had ceased, they still stood in brilliant light. The leader (he wore a garment of gold and silver) stepped forward and addressed us. He said the gathering had been arranged for us ages ago – long before we had left his world of light – to dwell for a space of time in the shadows of the earth plane. He hoped we would continue to seek our chosen pathways, and that the healing experience we had witnessed would always stay evergreen in our minds. The leader went on to say when we reached the age of maturity that some of us, when administering to the sick, would know that the healing rays of gold, silver and the colours of the rainbow were always available.

He bade us farewell, touching each one of us lightly on our heads, and blessed us. Before I returned to the awakened state, I remember taking a last look around the hall, absorbing the equisite beauty and splendour of it all. When we left, the walls were still vibrating with gold and silver, merging one with the other. The Mother of Pearl moved constantly in the endless depths and heights, top and bottom.

Through the years, I have more than once wished to return to that lovely hall in the spiritual spheres. It was not to be. But everything which took place there is so imprinted in my mind, I shall never forget it. One day, if I am left with enough time, I hope to paint that superb experience of teaching. It has indeed stayed evergreen in my mind.

Although at that time I had become aware of Charlie Kemp during previous spiritual visits, I was not conscious of him at all during the "gold and silver gathering." No doubt he also had lessons to learn elsewhere.

Not many people realise that the spiritual inspirers, advisers, teachers, and so many others also receive training in the spirit world to enable them to work in attunement with their channels residing in the physical body. Mediums and healers do likewise on the earth plane by sitting for meditation and in classes for the development of their psychic and spiritual gifts, in addition to visiting the spirit world for instruction.

I often look back on my early spiritual visits and think how fortunate I was. I still, on occasions, go through the curtain for what I call refresher courses on animal healing with our beloved Charlie Kemp. As before, I do not always remember everything that has taken place during "training behind the scenes," but I know the knowledge gained when the need arises when I give healing to a sick animal will always be brought to the fore.

Tessa Martindale

MRS. MARTINDALE wrote for help, explaining: "Tessa, my pony, has been troubled by a very distressing cough this entire winter. Any effort on her part makes her breath laboured. Yesterday, I noted that she was softly but audibly breathing. It should not be possible to hear a horse breathe normally."

"Tessa has very congested lungs, and suffers with bronchitis," said Charlie, who promised to help her with absent healing.

The pony responded to the healing for some months later, Mrs. Martindale wrote to say, "Tessa is now sound." At the same time, Sandy, Mrs. Martindale's donkey, was also placed on absent healing for bad breath and a growth on her side.

I remember going to sleep one night and joining Charlie in the spirit world, then leaving with him and his group of students to make our way to the field where Sandy had her stable. When we all arrived she was standing up in it, and seemed to me to be waiting to greet us for she butted Charlie warmly and gently with her head. Charlie said to her, "You knew we were coming to see you, didn't you?" He asked her to turn round so we could all see the side that was affected. Sandy did so. I sensed she knew Charlie was going to help her by the way she lovingly looked at him.

What happened next was astonishing. A white mist appeared slowly from Charlie's hands. Directed about six inches away from Sandy's growth, the mist gradually formed into a column, and I became aware of the great healing energy within it. The students and I were fascinated as we watched Charlie move the column up and down and side to side over the growth. The movements reminded me of the sign of the cross. After a short while, the column broke up into small white clouds with tinges of blue in them. They rotated around Sandy and became thicker in density until we could hardly see her. The stable was filled with the clouds. I felt I was standing in a very pleasant fog, enjoying it thoroughly.

Then it all cleared away quickly. I thought after all that Sandy's growth must have disappeared. But no, it was still there. I could not see any difference. Charlie was aware of my thoughts. He smiled, and said to Sandy, "We will wait and see what happens." Then I suddenly woke up.

In due course, a note arrived from Mrs. Martindale, saying: "Since you started absent healing on Sandy, the growth on her ribs has shrunk to roughly a third of the size it was. It is now the size of an almond nut."

Later came, "I would like to express my gratitude for the fact that the growth on Sandy's side, which was the size of a goose egg, has become non-existent."

I sent out a few words of thanks to our beloved Charlie for allowing me the privilege of witnessing him "in action." Indeed, it was a great honour.

Tara Sulerman

TARA, at eleven weeks old, was a sickly, and a very weak little King Charles Cavalier Spaniel, when she was bought and given as a Christmas present to Mrs. Sulerman, who naturally was extremely worried over Tara's terrible condition. When she arrived at the centre, I thought the stakes for her survival on earth were not very high. Tara was not eating at all, and was very thin.

Her vet informed Mrs. Sulerman that Tara would eat when she was ready. As time went on, and she still was not eating and getting thinner, Mrs. Sulerman decided to bring her to us for contact healing.

Charlie, with Spot by his side, soon arrived. Spot jumped up onto our table and lay down beside Tara to comfort her. She tried to wag her little tail in greeting to him.

Charlie looked over Tara and said to us, "This little soul was born with a deformity and has a blockage, both in the intestine and her stomach." I went into trance with him, and watched while he operated on Tara's stomach. He seemed to split a substance apart, and then smoothed down the sides of it. Further along the intestine, there was a ball of black matter which Charlie proceeded to treat with a red ray. I watched the blockage crumble away. The whole procedure only took a few minutes.

I heard Charlie request Gerald after the operation to give Tara a soft centred chocolate to eat. We do not normally have chocolates in stock, but it so happened that being Christmas time we had been given a box. Charlie mentioned that Tara would now start to eat. Gerald gave her a lovely big chocolate, which she ate ravenously, and asked for more! By this time Spot was standing up, cheering her on. From that date to this Tara has not looked back. She has a very healthy appetite.

When Tara was bought from the kennels, the Sulermans

were given to understand she was twelve weeks old. Charlie stated she was, in fact, nine weeks old. Tara's own vet later confirmed this.

During a recent phone talk with Mrs. Sulerman, she said that Tara "is very healthy, eating very well and loves her chocs!" No doubt these are the expensive kind. She must be five years old now, bless her.

Lucy Churchill

POOR Lucy was indeed suffering not physically, but mentally, for she was very jealous of Sophie, her companion at home. Both are Springer Cocker Spaniels. Lucy is temperamental in addition.

It so happened that Sophie was a little off colour, and therefore not so assertive in their relationship as was her wont. Her failing in this matter gave Lucy the opportunity to become very aggressive towards her, and try to attack her.

When her owner, Richard and Mary Churchill, brought Lucy to us for contact healing, I felt the torment within her. She had the look of jealousy. It was in her eyes.

Charlie did not promise to change Lucy's character or temperament, but stated he would just help her to relax her mind. Physically she was very healthy. We gently laid our hands on her head.

Soon after, Mrs. Churchill reported that Lucy was on her best behaviour, and that her aggressive attitude towards Sophie had changed. Sophie had also recovered – and was the boss once again. The environment was very peaceful!

Charlie mentioned afterwards to me how animals are like human beings. When weakness is shown, if given the chance the bully will attack. I could not help but agree.

Pash Green

"WE are praying that you may be able to help our dog through absent healing. He is a Tibetan Shihtzu, answers to the name of Pash, and is five years old. We gave him a home, but he has always suffered from this awful biting and scratching. We thought it was nerves, but our vet says it is an allergy, and cannot find the cause.

"Pash has anti-inflammatory injections and drugs most of the time, which give him a very little ease, until it all starts again. It is going on at the moment!" So wrote Mr. and Mrs. Green.

Charlie advised for Pash to have fresh food, and one teaspoon of honey morning and night. Meantime absent healing would continue. Mr. and Mrs. Green replied: "Pash does have fresh meat, but has never been easy to feed, not being our pet until fourteen months old. We have tried many times and in different ways, but he will not look at honey."

Examining his photograph, Pash seems a lovely little fellow. Judging by the delightful, smiling, happy faces of his owners, he is very fortunate and well loved.

Charlie was not perturbed by the refusal of Pash to take honey, but simply said, "I will look after him just the same." When I asked Charlie what he thought caused Pash's allergy he said, "It could well be the chemicals man puts into the drinking water."

Some weeks afterwards a note from Mr. and Mrs. Green arrived, saying: "The allergy has gone which affected Pash's back. We all pray it will not return." We did not hear any more.

However, Charlie did mention that Pash's allergy was "difficult." He hoped it would not return, but owing to the nature of it there was a possibility it might, but he would always try to keep it at bay.

Chapter 5
The Painted Lady

I WAS born and lived my childhood in London, in a tenement house located in Southam Street, North Kensington, not far from the now very well-known Portobello Road. It was a tough and very poor district indeed where bed bugs, cockroaches and rats resided in abundance. They were part and parcel of family life. There were no tenant's rights in those days or security of tenure. And no one dared to complain about the dreadful conditions either.

My parents rented rooms – a kitchen with a blackleaded stove, a scullery in the basement with an old stone copper, and three rooms on the ground floor. Two were used as bedrooms and the other one as the parlour – the best room – which was sacred. We were never allowed to go into it unattended – not that there was much in the room – but it was always kept for visitors. The property, by today's standards, would have been condemned and demolished on sight. It was also terribly damp, with an awful musty smell and mildew on most of the walls.

We certainly had our share of rats, not just one or two, but many. They took up residence not only in the coal cellar in our area, but had planned and worked out clear runways from one tenement house to another underground. It was a positive Mafia of the rodent world!

The rats were everywhere. It was not unusual to see them walking sedately together and without fear along the gutters in the road, more so on a Sunday afternoon. Those were the days. However, although we were to a certain degree accustomed to the rats in the coal cellar, they instinctively knew that our living accommodation was out of bounds to them, for whenever a bold rat ventured forth into the kitchen or other parts of our home, they soon learnt to their cost that they would never be given the chance to do it again.

Many a time I saw my mother armed with the copper stick – it was very heavy and about two-and-a-half feet in length and six inches in diameter – chase a rat around until she cornered it and was able to thump it until it was dead.

The coal cellar was more a home for these creatures than for holding coal as my parents could not afford to have a full cellar. We were lucky to have a little coal from time to time so the rats had a field day. We could always hear them squeaking and fighting amongst themselves.

Writing about rats, brings back to my mind the incident of the "King Rat." We named him Freddie – and I have never seen one so large. He was enormous, jet black in colour, very cocky indeed, cunning and deadly but with great courage for he dared to go where angels feared to tread . . . indoors!

We had heard of Freddie's prowess and stunts from neighbours, who appeared to be scared to death of him. When it suited him, he would go into their homes and be discovered sitting on their kitchen tables or wooden boxes which were often used in those days for same, with two or three of his cronies. When approached, he was always aggressive, spat at the neighbours, then made an easy get away.

My mother and father acquired a rat trap in the form of a cage and would leave it out on alternate nights. As the rats sensed it was a danger to them, it would be camouflaged. Sometimes in the morning there were one, two or three rats in the cage, but not always for they were very wily and crafty. They soon realised that to stay alive it was wise not to touch the rat poison which had been laid down. It really was a constant battle of wits between us.

One hot summer's day, my mother apparently walked into her kitchen, a most sacred place to her. Sitting on the dresser with impunity and as large as life was King Rat. She rushed out to the scullery to get the stick. The impudent creature did not make a move until she was about to hit him on the top of the head. Mother said it sat there staring her out! He got away, much to her dismay and temper. By that time, Mother made up her mind to get him – come what may.

I came home from school to see her washing down the dresser with disinfectant, which was always handy. Afterwards she got carried away by washing over everything in sight: in the kitchen, old bits of furniture; the table (which was meticulously scrubbed) chairs – the few that we had – all the china, and even the cutlery, which was in the kitchen drawer. I am sure mother must have thought Freddie had sorted out a knife and fork for himself to eat a meal. Then, last but not least, the lino on the kitchen floor was soaked in disinfectant. Needless to say, we all had to wait for tea – which was near supper time when we got it.

So out came the rat cage once again with a lump of cheese, which my parents could ill afford. By this time, all the neighbours had heard through the grapevine about Freddie's visit to our house and my mother's anger and determination to kill him. Quite a few knocked at our door to give what they thought good, sound advice and instructions on how to capture him. These were remarks which, frankly, I thought would have been better left unsaid for my dear mother, not prone to beat about the bush, promptly replied: "Why don't you all practise what you preach? You have had the opportunity to do so. I don't need any of you to set the bullets for me to fire!" That was the end of forthcoming advice and helping hands.

This all happened at a time when my father was lucky enough to have a few week's work. However, on three alternate nights when the cage was put out in the area, only three small rats were inside it. There was no sign of Freddie; he was far too clever and cunning to fall for that ploy. My mother, I knew, would not give up, and was prepared to wait a few days. Early one morning as she went out into the area, there was King Rat sitting on the steps, looking at her. Once again, she rushed indoors to get her copper stick. Freddie did not move until she was on the point of hitting him. How he must have laughed at her!

Well, by this time things were really beyond a joke. Mother was furious and became more determined than ever to get him so started to work out her strategy regarding the capture of Freddie. On the scene at that time of my life were loyal and trusted friends of my parents, Mr. and Mrs. Arthur Edwards. Mr. Edwards was an old army colleague of my father's in the 1914–1918 war. The Edwards' lived a few streets away from us. They would call twice a week, mainly for Mr. Edwards to play a game of dominoes with Dad. My parents would return the visits the following week.

Unfortunately, poor Mr. Edwards had suffered appalling injuries which left him severely wounded, and badly shell shocked. This brought about a constant shaking of his head from side to side. His eyes were also affected: the pupils shook, his eyes suddenly crossing. I would mentally say to my dear spirit friends, "Please help Mr. Edwards to uncross his eyes again as he has got them tied up."

Mr Edwards' balance was dreadful. I often wondered how he managed to stand up, let alone walk. People who did not know him used to think he was drunk, but in fact, he was teetotal. And apart from all these disabilities, the poor man was also left with a terrible stutter, which caused him to take a very long time to utter a single word. Many a time I saw people when attempting to hold a conversation with him start to stutter themselves, not realising what they were doing in their endeavours to help him get his words out.

Nevertheless, Mr. Edwards and his wife, Carrie, were sweet, kindly souls and would always help others in need as much as possible. They were just as poor as we were.

It so happened they were present when the subject of King Rat was discussed, and the catching of him. Suddenly I heard a spirit voice say to me: "Irene, kind Mr. Edwards is going to offer your mother help in catching the rat. Tell her not to let him help her as he will not benefit by it." These words puzzled me then, but later it was putting it gently.

While my parents were talking, I saw a vision very clearly of my mother hitting Mr. Edwards on top of his head with her copper stick and knocking him out: she laid him out flat. Then I saw her bending over him – and the vision faded. I knew Spirit were warning me of the danger to come. What on earth was I to do? Knowing how angry my father would be if I interrupted the conversation, especially if I mentioned the spirit warning as well, I decided to stay quiet for a while and listen, hoping and praying that Mr. Edwards would stop and think twice before offering his services.

But no, the dear, kindly soul after much struggling stuttered, "Mmmmmmmrs. Cccclements. lll wwwill hhhit ttthe rrrat ffffor yyyyou aaaafter yyyyou hhhhave cccornered hhhhim." I thought he was certainly pushing his luck too far as he had to hold a newspaper about a quarter of an inch from his eyes to read it, then he could only read the large print and his wife would read the rest for him. I could see my mother was wondering how to refuse his offer without hurting his feelings, but Mr. Edwards was determined to help her. Finally, Mother agreed on condition he cornered the rat and she would hit it. I thought, "Oh God, she is being optimistic as she knows the state of him." Since those days I have often wished I had a movie camera then, knowing the outcome of their combined efforts.

I began to get frantic and frightened for Mr. Edwards, so mentally called out to my spirit friends to try to change his mind, which I knew was impossible, as we all have to use our own freewill. Once again, I heard the voice telling me to warn my mother of the danger, and had a re-run of the vision. So I plucked up courage and said as loud as I could: "Mum, I have heard a voice tell me you are not to let Mr. Edwards help you. I have seen a vision and saw you knock him out with your copper stick."

There was an unusual silence. My parents became embarrassed by my outburst. Father severely reprimanded me and threatened to send me to bed if I interfered again and did not behave myself. Dear Mr. Edwards felt sorry for me. I shall always remember his words to me: "Iiiiirene, lllllittle gggirl. YYYou mmust not wworry oon mmm my aacount. Yyyour dddear mmmother wwould nnot hhhurt mmme. Ssshe would nnot hhhurt aa fff ffly. Wwe ttt together, yyyou ss see, wwill catch the rat." Obviously he was not aware of the strength of my mum when armed with a copper stick and in action. I promptly burst into floods of tears. Mr. Edwards drew me close to him and cuddled me.

I remember quite well that the only one who paid a little attention to my warning, although she was very careful not to refer to it, was little Mrs. Edwards. She tackled the problem in her gentle, quiet way by saying to her husband, "You know, Arthur dear, you may not feel well enough in the morning to come and help Mrs. Clements, as it takes you some time to get your faculties into focus." I could not stop crying for I knew he certainly would not be well enough after the event. But he was adamant, and stood his ground. By this time, my father had had enough of me bawling, so I was quickly sent to bed, where I earnestly prayed that something would happen to prevent Mr. Edwards from getting hurt.

I became aware of my spiritual friends in the bedroom. One lady sat on my bed and said to me: "There is nothing more you can do. We will do all we can to help, but everyone on the earth plane is responsible for their words, actions and deeds and must always decide for themselves. If your mother and Mr. Edwards choose to go into battle together to catch the rat it is their choice entirely. You have given them our warning."

The next day dawned. Mr. Edwards, brought by his wife, arrived at 8.00 am. Mrs. Edwards, not being a lover of rats, wisely decided to return home. Father had left for work whilst I had started my school holiday. Mother was all ready with her fighting plans. So the scene was set. I remember Mr. Edwards saying he felt as bright as a button – I thought, "You won't be for much longer!" – and that he knew all would go well.

We went over the plans several times. I was to keep watch for Freddie at the kitchen window, which looked out onto the area. Dear Mr. Edwards was to sit on the chair until the alarm call came. Mother would be carrying out household jobs until I whispered to her that Freddie had arrived. The copper stick was behind the door. When I gave the signal, my mum and her staunch, brave friend, were going to creep along the dark passageway. They were dim in the tenement houses in those days since there was no electricity, and reminded me of narrow tunnels. Then Mother, armed with the copper stick, would gently open the door that led to the area. Mr. Edwards was to follow quietly, a foolhardy idea if ever there was one.

The plan, I thought, was understood and put into operation. After a while – it seemed a long time waiting – Freddie suddenly appeared and sat on the bottom one of the steps. I whispered, "Quick, Mum, Freddie is here." She very swiftly moved out of the kitchen. Mr. Edwards tried to get up, but somehow managed to fall off his chair. I helped him up and propelled him through the door, with forebodings, into the passage. Then I returned to the kitchen window. Within seconds, there was such a hullabaloo going on in the passageway, with bumping and thumping. Next I heard Mr. Edwards making loud noises. I heard him stutter out quite clearly: "Mrs. Clements, where are you? Where is the area?" The poor man, not being able to see anyway, had turned round in the dark and got hopelessly lost, points which my mum had overlooked.

Needless to say, the rat had ample warning to escape, which he did. I collapsed in fits, laughing, which did not please my mother or improve the tense situation that soon developed, or her temper.

A few minutes afterwards, she had obviously thought things out very carefully and kindly said: "Mr. Edwards, we do appreciate very much you taking the trouble to help us, but there really is no need for you to put yourself at risk or bother any more regarding the rat. I shall be quite all right. Please let Irene take you home now." After a lot of persuasion, he agreed. As I walked him home, I thanked my spirit friends for saving the day - as I thought then - and for returning him to a very relieved wife.

We all thought that was that, but the next morning promptly at 8.00 am. the Edwards' arrived. He was bubbling over with enthusiasm for the day's events; she, although not expressed, was full of misgivings, as there was every right to be under the circumstances.

We all realised not only did my mum have a problem regarding the rat, but with her "Little Helper" as well. What was she to do with him? It was a headache, not only for her but for me also as I already knew the outcome . . . worse still for Mr Edwards!

In the end, my mother decided to stand Mr. Edwards behind the rear door, which I did not think was a wise decision, but dare not say so. Poor man, he stood behind the door every day for many hours all week, only leaving his post when nature called, or to spend a few minutes being fortified by only a cup of tea. Then I would walk him home in the evenings.

Much to my amusement, I thought it might have helped to hang him up by his collar on the hook on the door, but my sense of humour was not shared by my parents.

However, I loved and admired dear Mr. Edwards, for what he lacked in physical attributes he certainly made up for with grit, courage and stamina. He showed me the true meaning of dedication.

There was no sign whatsoever during the week of Freddie. To be truthful, I was bored with having constantly to keep watch. I hated wasting time (and still do) but had to do as I was told. On several occasions I asked my spirit friends to send the rat away, talk to it and tell it to go, but it is not as easy as that for Spirit to agree to our requests.

The seventh morning dawned. We were all on guard. Mother, as usual, had thrown out several small pieces of bread to entice Freddie. Although on this occasion I did not see him arrive, suddenly I saw him in a corner of the area sitting up, eating a piece of bread. He had obviously relaxed his guard and was feeling pretty hungry. I whispered to mother, "Freddie is outside sitting comfortably." She crept along the passageway. I was in time to see Mr. Edwards take hold of my mother's skirt as she went past him. I remember thinking, "That is the last thing she wants, to be held back." I moved silently behind them, praying to God not to let "it" happen.

Mother must have sensed Mr. Edwards was going to get in the way. As she picked up her copper stick, she quietly opened the door and said to him: "Stay where you are. Don't move!" Then the action started. Into battle went my mum, copper stick held high towards Freddie, who instantly knew war had been declared.

I was pleased to see Mr. Edwards appeared to be having a fight with the open door and decided to let him carry on doing so as it was safer for him.

But it was not to last. Hearing the clarion call seemed to spur him on to the rescue of my dear mum, though, knowing her, she really did not need to be rescued. Round and round the area went the rat, stopping to spit every so often at mother, who was by then unstoppable, wielding her copper stick in all directions and hitting her foe several times. But still he kept going. Unfortunately, so did Mr. Edwards, who was blindly following mother around, heedless of her repeated warnings.

She shouted out to him to keep clear. I knew she wasn't talking to the rat, who went into a corner, spitting for all he was worth, looking extremely menacing. Mr. Edwards could not see, and chose the same corner at the same time.

He was felled a mighty blow on the top of his head with the copper stick, which completely knocked him out. I can still see my fearless mum thumping at the rat until it was dead, over poor Mr. Edward's body. For a moment or two I thought he was dead as well for he looked such a ghastly colour, and was turning mauve. I remember thinking, "I wonder if he is going like that all over."

Then I heard a spirit voice say: "Little one, run for help. You must get the injured one lifted inside for he will have a dreadful headache." I thought, "Not much!" I recall replying to the voice, "By the look of him, you may have to lift him upstairs." The voice reassured me that in time he would be all right.

I rushed next door for help, leaving mother terribly upset, crying, trying to get Mr. Edwards back to a conscious state, but he was out for the count. Finally, with the help of two burly male neighbours – it was a blessing then they were unemployed – they got him back into our home.

Mr Edwards did look funny for he had a huge bump on his head, larger than a duck's egg. The men laid him out on the kitchen floor. One of them went and brought down the mattress and pillow off my bed. They gently lifted Mr. Edwards onto the mattress. I remember thinking how gentle one of the men was when he lifted Mr. Edwards' head onto the pillow.

He was far too ill to be moved. Nobody thought of calling a doctor. Anyway they could not be afforded, not where we lived. Our district would have fitted well into a Charles Dickens' story. As I stood looking down at him feeling dreadfully sorry, I thought that if only he and Mother had taken the spirit warning instead of shutting their ears to it, he would not have been lying there knocked out. It could have been avoided.

Once again I heard the spirit voice talking to me, saying, "Little one, hold the sick man's hands and we will administer healing to him." I did this for a few minutes, hoping mother would not notice. She did not because she was in such a dreadful state. Suddenly she remembered to send me round to Mrs. Edwards. I ran all the way, and knocked at the front door. I could hear Mrs. Edwards singing as she came down the stairs into the hall and felt awful as I knew she would not be singing for long. As soon as she opened the door she said: "It's Arthur. I knew it!" She held on to the door for support. I thought, "Oh God, if she is going to be like this now, what will she be like when she sees him?"

Mrs Edwards cried all the way back to my home. When we got into the kitchen, she took one look at her husband and promptly fainted. As there was such panic going on, nobody took any notice of her. There she lay. Mother was stepping backwards and forwards over her, running to the kitchen sink with a towel soaked in cold water to put on the bump on Mr. Edwards' head, which seemed to me to be getting bigger.

Suddenly one of the men realised Mrs. Edwards was on the floor. He and the other one carefully picked her up (she looked like a little rag doll) and laid her along the side of the wall by the kitchen sink, where I thought a few splashes of cold water, through Mother's frantic activities, might help to revive her. We certainly could have done with some ice cubes in those days, some for Mr. Edwards and his wife as well. I remember saying to my unseen friends, "Please hurry and get Mrs. Edwards awake as there is not enough room in this kitchen for one body, let alone two."

News, good or bad, always travelled fast through the grapevine in our district. It was not long before the neighbours got to hear of the day's dreadful happening, the tragic accident to the Clements' good friend. Gradually, they came to pay their respects to him. He did look as though he was lying in state, stretched out and with no apparent sign of life. But they also wanted to congratulate mother on her victory and witness the evidence of the murdered Freddie, which was not a pretty sight. Some of the neighbours turned up with pieces of old clothing, which was torn up to act as bandages for Mr. Edwards' head, which was bleeding.

I shall never forget one woman, who always seemed to feed her family on pig's trotters. She arrived with one already cooked on a very cracked plate. She stuck it under Mr. Edwards' nose and exclaimed: "Come on Mr. Edwards. 'Ere, get this down yer! Yer'll feel a lot better." I failed to see how, and thought, "If he opens his eyes and sees that awful mess in front of him, it will finish him off altogether."

Mother gently moved her and the pig's trotter away from him.

Other neighbours came in, some with broken biscuits, or two or three teaspoons of tea, whatever they could spare. One arrived with a tiny lamb chop, which I am sure was meant to be for her husband's dinner. Small amounts of sugar and milk were handed in, a few slices of bread, some potatoes, a few pieces of streaky bacon and other edible items. I remember thinking how I would love to have the small pot of raspberry jam that was amongst the goodies when I felt a spirit hand lightly touching my shoulder. A voice whispered to me: "Irene, Mr. Edwards' needs are greater than yours. You will have all the raspberry jam you want later in life." Thinking about that, and taking into account my very young age and that I would have to wait an awful long time, I wasn't too sure. But I did feel ashamed for allowing such thoughts to enter my head. However, I must admit I was sorely tempted!

As the gifts arrived, the donors placed them all around Mr. Edwards, who was still out flat. I had a fit of the giggles for some kind soul had put a packet of senna pods near him. I thought, "That is the last thing he is going to need or anybody else in this room, come to that." One gloomy soul – there is always one around in times of crisis – arrived with a huge bunch of white lilies. God knows where she got them from for in those days they were used mostly for funerals and weddings.

When she placed them at Mr. Edwards' feet that was the last straw for me. I did my best to stop laughing out loud, though it was difficult. The expression on my face must have looked peculiar! Mother quickly removed the flowers, saying to the woman, "Mr. Edwards has not yet reached the stage where he will be willing to accept them." This caused me to go into uncontrollable laughter for I was not sure which way she thought he was going! My brand of humour was not shared by anyone in the kitchen, least of all little Mrs. Edwards, who by this time had managed to drag herself up from the floor and was sitting holding her husband's hands. She caught sight of the lilies, which instantly reduced her to floods of tears. She berated the lily-bearer, calling her a "ghoul" who was only happy when she could enjoy a funeral.

I had never before seen Mrs. Edwards in such fighting form. In fact, I did not think she had it in her. One should not be surprised really by the actions of others in times of emergencies and when under stress, but Mrs. Edwards was determined to protect her loved one – come what might. And so the angry discussion raged on until the lily-bearer said, "By the look of 'im, 'e would be better off dead." I remember thinking that although the lily-bearer had not physically knocked out Mrs. Edwards, she had certainly rendered her speechless; she was terribly shocked by the unkind words. In fact, everyone was upset by the statement. For a moment or two, Mother did not quite know how to handle the situation.

After an uncomfortable silence of a few minutes, attention was returned to the unconscious form. I mistakenly thought it might cheer up Mrs. Edwards by saying to her, "If God called Mr. Edwards he will not die anyway, for he will only have left his body behind." Unfortunately for me, the effect on her was disastrous: she had hysterics. I was swiftly pushed out of the kitchen by Mother, and informed I was not to return unless I behaved myself.

Some time later that evening, the good neighbours were still sitting around Mr. Edwards, who had not stirred. I touched him several times and was aware of spirit friends very close to me. By the intense heat from my hands I knew he was receiving help from us.

There was a knock at the door. I went and opened it. There stood a woman, but it was not until many years afterwards that I realised she was a lady of easy virtue. She lived in the next street to us. I had spoken to her on several occasions as she had a great love for all animals. She would often pass the time of day with me and my young friends. We always looked forward to what we called her "sweetie bag" which she carried with her. It was full of sweets and chocolates for us to share, a great treat, and a rare luxury for us.

All her animals loved her. She had many dogs – all different breeds – and cats. All were extremely well fed and healthy.

One day, I met her walking with two of her dogs along the street. As my parents were not with me, I felt free to ask questions. But I did ask her first if she would mind me asking her them, in case Mum got to find out what I was up to via the grapevine. I remember the "Painted Lady," for she was such, owing to the heavy make up she wore, looking kindly down at me and replying: "Of course I don't mind. If you don't ask, you don't get the answers. What is it you want to know?"

I plucked up courage and boldly ventured forth with: "How do you manage to keep all your dogs and cats? Where do you get them from?" She smiled at me and said her uncles gave them to her. I replied: "You must have lots of uncles then. Do they always give you a dog or a cat?" She laughed out loud, and said, "No dearie, not exactly."

In my total ignorance and innocence I pushed the questioning further by saying, "What do you mean, by 'Not exactly?' What do they give you then?" She became more amused than ever and laughingly replied, "Always a trinket, just a little trinket." She then tapped me lovingly on the top of my head and went on her way chuckling.

I had previously noticed on many occasions that the local wives and mothers would always steer clear of her if they saw her walking towards them. I often saw them cross over to the other side of the road to avoid her. I used to think it was strange, but it never bothered me or their cold behaviour, and did not give it a second thought. Mother would always speak to her when the necessity arose, but nevertheless I was not sure whether or not she would be welcome in our home.

There she stood with one of her dogs outside our door, with a large bottle of gin in one hand, a beautiful crystal glass in the other. I could not help but wonder where she had got them from. I was in a quandry. I stood looking at her for a few seconds and then heard her say, "Can I come in, dearie?" I thought I had better ask Mum first. So I returned to the kitchen and said to her: "The lady with the painted face is here with a bottle of spirits for Mr. Edwards. She wants to come in. Shall I let her?"

I saw the look of horror on the neighbours' faces as they started to whisper amongst themselves and to fidget. My parents instantly agreed that as she had taken the trouble to visit us, she must be allowed to come in, so she did. And the scene which followed was hilarious, one I shall never forget. It is as vivid today in my memory as it was then.

As the "Painted Lady" drew close to Mr. Edwards, the women moved away from her with a considerable amount of tutt-tutting. She asked mother for a saucer as she wanted to give her little dog a drop of gin. Apparently, some of her dogs and cats – not all – always had their little nightcap of gin since she said, "It does 'em good and gets 'em used to strangers at night," a remark I was to ponder upon many times. What with all of her uncles and strangers as well, I could not make things fit. Still, it was none of my business. I knew it would not be any good asking my parents to explain; they would not give me the key to the puzzle!

The dog was called Bruno, but did not match his name owing to the fact he was a Yorkshire terrier. If ever there was a misfit, he was it! He sat up on his hind legs and watched his mistress pour out the gin into his saucer. I must say he drank it very quickly, and lay down beside her. Everyone was astonished, and could not believe their eyes. The "Painted Lady" then poured more gin into the lovely crystal glass. I was fascinated by the beautiful colours that emanated from it; they reminded me of the hues I had seen so many times during my visits to the spirit world. She placed the glass under Mr. Edwards' nose despite Mrs. Edwards' protests that her husband "is tee-total, and has not touched a drop in his life." This made me wonder if it was due to the lack of opportunity, short of cash, or did he definitely have no taste for it? I could see that Mrs. Edwards, who had not stopped crying all evening, was going to enter a state of hysteria again as she continued that "If Arthur has a drop of that foul stuff it will finish him off altogether." I thought it might jerk him back to the conscious state, and voiced my opinion out loud, not that anybody took any notice. The problem was this: how would it be possible to get him to take it – he was still out cold – unless his mouth was forced open and the gin was poured down his throat, but I could not see that happening.

The "Painted Lady" was getting fed up with Mrs. Edwards' clinging onto her arm so said to her: " 'Ere Dearie, this stuff is quite 'armless. It's not so bad as yer think. It'll calm yer nerves after what yer 'ave been through. Yer need it. 'Ere take it. It'll 'elp yer." We all looked in amazement as the irate one took hold of the glass and in one go gulped down the tot of gin! I anxiously waited for the results. They soon came, for Mrs. Edwards gave one shriek and started to run round the kitchen in circles, gasping for breath, unable to speak. I heard a spirit voice say to me: "Quickly! Get the stricken one a jug of water and give it to her, all of it to drink, and place your hands on her abdomen." I thought that under the circumstances this was a tall order for me to be able to carry out, especially as my Father was present.

I decided to do as I was told, and if necessary to explain afterwards. Regardless of where I thought poor Mrs. Edwards was going to put it all, I filled up an enamel jug which held a gallon of water, stopped her in her tracks, gave her the jug and grabbed hold of a chair. I knew that spirit friends were behind the scene for Mrs. Edwards quietly collapsed onto it, holding the jug tightly to her chest, which I am sure she thought would be her life saver. She frantically drank the water, spilling quite a lot of it down her dress because the jug was so large. I wondered when Mrs. Edwards was going to come up for air so that I could place my hands on her stomach. She paused for a moment and moved the jug slightly – which seemed to me to be sitting on her lap – but I was able to place my hands on her as Spirit had requested. As I did so, I saw several pairs of spirit hands moving in rotation over Mrs. Edwards head, chest and stomach. From their hands flowed forth a brilliant turquoise-blue colour. I had the impression it was as light as gossamer. I felt not only intense heat coming from my hands as I touched Mrs. Edwards, but also from the turquoise colour, which I know now to be one of the main healing energies from the spirit world.

To those who do not understand spirit healing, a spiritual healer is the instrument for the Spirit to contact to enable them to administer healing energies to those in need. I watched as the hands gently moved over Mrs. Edwards and noticed she was becoming drowsy. Her head drooped. In a loud voice, one of the female neighbours declared, "She's boozed!"

Thankfully, no one took any notice. They just stood waiting to see what would happen next with her. After a few minutes I watched the hands gradually disappear, taking the turquoise-blue healing energy with them. Then

Mrs. Edwards slowly lifted up her head, opened her eyes and exclaimed: "Where have the doctor and nurses gone? There were four nurses. They were all so nice to me. They all spoke to me, including the doctor, when they touched me. I feel absolutely free now. It's funny because I thought and felt before they came that I had had too much to drink. How silly one can get!"

Mrs. Edwards had, in fact, seen the doctor and nurses from the Other Side, but I did not deem it wise to confirm it at that moment of time. As I looked at her, I realised she had regained her composure. The panic had gone, her breathing was normal and she had her wits about her. I mentally thanked my dear spirit friends for they had done a grand job.

The excitement of Mrs. Edwards' performance now over, attention once again was given to Mr. Edwards' recumbent form. The "Painted Lady" had poured more gin out into the glass and was holding it under his nose. After receiving no response whatsoever from him, she drank it, declaring, "It can't be wasted!" These actions were repeated several times, much to my parents' concern, and that of others who were present. I whispered to mother: "Why doesn't she pour the gin back into the bottle? Why does she think she is wasting it?" Mother did not reply. I could see she was very anxious about the outcome. My main worry was that I desperately hoped that during the course of these many tipples, the "Painted Lady" would not include Bruno, but she did!

To have a drunken "Painted Lady" was one thing, but to have a drunken dog and an unconscious Mr. Edwards as well was going to be too much for anyone to bear. I sent out urgent thoughts for help to my friends. Although at that moment of time I could not see them, I felt they were close by.

By this time, the "Painted Lady" had become grotesque. She was red in the face. Perspiration was running down it, making little streams, through her thickly plastered make-up. Her eye mascara had merged into the rouge on her cheeks, and she looked as though she had two black eyes. I could not help thinking she reminded me of a clown, and a very sad one. I felt so dreadfully sorry for her, although at the time I did not really understand the reason why.

However, the pantomine was not to last for much longer, for the "Painted Lady" was beginning to lose her balance. She stood, lurched over Mr. Edwards and started to hiccup, saying to him: "I'm so sorry to see yer like this. I just wanted to 'elp yer." I thought at the time if anyone needed the help, she certainly did! She then burst forth into song with, "She's only a bird in a gilded cage." I must admit she did have a lovely voice even if she was tipsy. The dog got up and joined in for all he was worth: obviously he was quite used to these sessions.

My parents had had enough . . . and so had the others in the kitchen. To be truthful, I thought it was quite good entertainment as it needed something to liven things up a bit. I was very amused, to say the least. Mother and father gently led the "Painted Lady" away, complete with glass and bottle. They propelled her out of the kitchen, still singing, followed by the dog, still howling, along the passageway, and out through the door and up to the top of the steps, where one of her "Uncles" was waiting for her. He carefully supported her across the road into "The Craven" public house opposite. I remember thinking that as she was already in a drunken state she would no doubt be carried out later that night. It would not have been the first time I had seen that happen to her.

Every Saturday night, it was not unusual for a Black Maria to drive up to the public house. The police waited to load up the drunks, who would come out fighting amongst themselves when "Time!" was called. In fact, it was our only entertainment, free for the locals, including the kids, to watch. There was no television in those days and hardly anyone could afford to go to the cinema to see a film so the pub frolics were more than welcome. Many times the "Painted Lady" was to be seen either being pushed or lifted with many others into the police van and driven off.

For some reason or other, once inside the van, the occupants would stop fighting and start singing at the tops of their voices. One thing I did notice was that the "Painted Lady" would never leave any of her dogs behind, which always pleased me a great deal. I often used to wonder why it was they never seemed to stand or walk firmly on their legs. They appeared to stagger and totter as they followed her into the police van, but after witnessing Bruno consuming several gin tipples, I had discovered the answer!

My parents and I returned to the kitchen. Pandemonium had broken out. Mrs. Edwards had again been reduced to floods of tears because of Bruno's howling which convinced her that her Arthur was going to die after all; admittedly his chances of survival did not appear to be very good. Needless to say, she was being aided and abetted by the "ghoul" who had previously upset her. She was telling Mrs. Edwards that she knew of an undertaker who would "bury 'im cheap. 'E can go in a public grave for after all, once yer gawn, yer gawn." Her advice certainly did not help the electric atmosphere which had developed.

Whenever a howling dog sat outside a particular house in our district or elsewhere, it inevitably meant that a passing to the Higher Life of someone would take place within a few days. As dogs are psychic, no doubt they are able to "see" something. Many people in days gone by considered a howling dog as an omen of death, one not to be taken lightly.

Although I could understand Mrs. Edwards' distress, I felt sure her husband was not due to be called Home at that moment of time, even if he did look very ill, for I could see the spirit doctor and the four nurses still attending to him. I remember feeling terribly hot while they were present.

Meantime, several women neighbours – I noticed not the men – were expressing their indignation regarding the "Painted Lady." That *she*, of all people should have been allowed to enter our home! I could not understand then why they were creating such a fuss, and thought they were being very unkind about her. My dear parents were in no mood to listen to their spiteful gossip. Mother quickly decided to put a stop to it, by saying very firmly: "Are we all so very different from each other? We all have faults and failings, skeletons in the cupboard somewhere along the line. None of us can afford to throw stones at another. I do know that God has noted her very kind action to help our friend. She came here in love. And as far as we are concerned, that is all that matters!" Come what may, I decided to join in and said in a very loud voice, "Yes, and the Spirit does not care who or what you are as long as you love your neighbours and wish to help them." There was an uncomfortable silence for a few minutes. This time I got away with it for I was not reprimanded by my father.

Mother's words had not evidently fallen on deaf ears for I noticed the female neighbours did later on manage to say "Hello" to the "Fallen One" whenever they happened to pass each other in the street. I was glad to see she was no longer an outcast. During the years I have often thought of the "Painted Lady" as the very kind lady with the trinkets. In fact, for a very long time I considered it a privilege to have known her and still do. At that time of my young life, although she was completely unaware of it, she helped me to widen my horizons in general. Come to think of it, she was without doubt rendering a valuable service to mankind, and, on reflection, at great cost.

After many hours, long into the evening, poor Mr. Edwards finally gained consciousness. He did not recognise any of us: he asked his wife who she was, and stared at us so vacantly we were all very upset. Father was overcome with emotion at seeing his dear old friend in what looked like a vegetable state for the rest of his life. He knelt down beside Mr Edwards and took hold of his hand. I am sure it was because he was in such a nervous state and so worried over his friend that he could not have realised what he was saying to him for Father asked if he would like to play a game of dominoes! I saw the funny side of it: others didn't. It had no effect on Mr. Edwards whatsoever. I could see the emotions of everyone in the kitchen were going down-hill rapidly.

I had been sitting very close to our friend and knew he was benefiting to a certain extent by my touching him when suddenly I felt myself being lifted off my chair and guided towards the middle of the kitchen. I stood there, wondering what I was doing. All the neighbours stopped talking. None of them had left during the day or the evening. They went for a few minutes to attend to various jobs in their homes and returned at intervals for they felt my parents needed their support, not unkindly I thought. Perhaps it may have been curiosity on their part, waiting to see which direction the Clements' friend was likely to travel!

I saw my spirit friends drawing close to me. One lady put her arm across my shoulder and said: "Little one, tell them to stay calm and not to despair for the dear friend will show signs of improvement in the morning. Regarding his memory, we need more time to restore him to a reasonable state of health, although under the circumstances it is impossible to help him back to normal health. We will make the best of what he has left. Tell them, Tell them. Do not be afraid to speak up. We are here with you. Inform your parents that at this moment of your time, the sick one is too ill to be moved. It is necessary and vital for him to stay in your home for three days, during which time we will continue to administer healing to him. Please continue to touch him by placing your hands upon him."

I was able, with spirit help, to relay the message as I received it to those in the kitchen and could see they were taken by surprise, even shock, including my parents. They looked at me in a very intense way. Father did not appear to be at all cross with me so I became more confident and decided to stand my ground by ending the message with "And my special friends are telling me to continue to touch Mr. Edwards with my hands." No one said a word: they all seemed to be stunned by my daring attitude, most of all mother and father. I returned quietly to my chair, thinking it best not to look at either of them, sat down beside our sick friend and held his hands. His eyes were open. Suddenly, he stuttered, "I have had a dream . . . a dream. I have been to a hospital. There were four nurses and a doctor. They were all looking at me and putting something on my head." That was all he said.

I knew he had seen the same spirit people as his wife and myself, but realised there would be no point in discussing the matter openly with those present.

Mother managed to get Mr. Edwards to take a little food, although he still had no idea who any of us were, but at least we were all thankful that he was alive – if only just. The neighbours went to their homes, promising to return the next day. They meant well, but I thought Mother would have preferred to do without them as she would be nursing a sick man. One of the male neighbours kindly walked Mrs. Edwards, who was exhausted, home. I must admit it was lovely and peaceful after everyone went.

I was sent up to bed. In the quiet of the bedroom, I felt the spiritual presence of my friends and remember saying to them: "I do so hope you will be able to get Mr. Edwards' memory back for him. We all do love him very much. If you can restore his memory, it will prove to my mum and dad and all the neighbours that you are there, won't it?" I was told to be patient and to wait and see until the morning.

The morning did not come quickly enough for me. It was dawn when I crept into the kitchen. Mother and Father were both asleep, sitting up in chairs since they had watched over their friend all night. He also was still stretched out asleep. I waited for a long time for them to wake up. Eventually they stirred, apart from Mr Edwards who appeared to be in a very deep sleep. Mother started to prepare Father's breakfast as he had to go to work. She went towards our friend with a cup of tea. I thought, "This is going to be the moment!" She woke him up: he moved and opened his eyes, but there was no spoken response from him. I was disappointed and knew my parents had not believed the spirit message to them the night before by the way they both looked at me. I helped Mr. Edwards to drink his tea. He had a little breakfast. Then he lay back, shut his eyes and appeared to go to sleep again. I noticed that the large bump on his head was considerably smaller. I sat close to him, and put my hands on him. Father left for work whilst Mother continued with some of her household duties which had been neglected.

During the morning, Mrs. Edwards came in. She was very dismayed to learn that her husband's condition was the same, but there were no tears. I think she had resigned herself to the possibility of her husband staying like he was for good. Several neighbours called with a look of expectancy on their faces: they were not able to hide their expressions when they discovered that the Clements' friend was still the same. I noticed they cast side glances at me, thinking that the Clements' had in their family a dotty kid – me!

Mother came into the kitchen to request in a very nice way for them to talk softly, as they could see Mr. Edwards was asleep. No sooner had she said that when suddenly he opened his eyes, sat up, glanced around at everyone, looked at me and stuttered, "Thank you, little one." Then he kissed me. "Mrs. Clements, you have given me a sore head, but please don't blame yourself," he said. "It was entirely my fault. Did you manage to get Freddie?"

Needless to say, there was great excitement all round.

Mrs. Edwards could not stop kissing her husband, who was trying to stutter to her that it seemed a long time to him since he had last seen her. There was much rejoicing. I remember Mother and Mrs. Edwards kneeling down together offering a prayer of thanks to God for the return of a very dear family friend and a very well-loved husband. As I watched them, my thoughts went back to the spirit warning prior to the accident. They had said that Mr. Edwards would be all right . . . and their words had come true.

As it was getting a bit too noisy in the kitchen and everyone seemed to be boiling over with happiness, Mother kindly suggested that all except Mrs. Edwards should return home. She thanked neighbours for their help during the very trying time. One by one they shook Mr. Edwards by the hand and quietly left.

When Father arrived home in the evening, walked into the kitchen and saw his old friend sitting up and talking to his wife, he was completely overcome. Father rushed over, put his arms around his neck and soundly kissed him, which resulted in Mr. Edwards doing the same to him. It was a touching reunion. I had never seen them kiss each other before or since. It was most unusual for Father as he was a man who always found it difficult openly to express emotion of any sort. I really don't know who was the most surprised, Mother, Mr. Edwards or his wife, but it was very funny. One can always see the funny side of life if it is looked for even in the most serious of situations. Mr. Edwards, not feeling well enough to go home, did stay with us for three days – as the Spirit had stated.

There were times when his memory was crystal clear yet on other occasions he had some difficulty in recognising us. I often reflected on the words of my spirit friends, "We will make the best of what he has left." Bless them: they had certainly done so.

Mother's terrific blow to his head had not improved Mr Edwards' ailments. It took him somewhat longer to get his words out whilst his head shook a little more. As time went by, our visits to his home became more frequent. But he was able to play many games of dominoes with Father just like they used to, albeit more slowly.

At the time of our friend's remarkable recovery, I really

did think that my parents, the neighbours and Mrs. Edwards would have wanted to have discussed the spirit message to them. I thought they would have been interested enough to ask questions about it, such as how was it possible for Mr. Edwards to recover as he did or how did the Spirit know he would have an improvement with his memory the following morning?

Their response was as dead as a dodo. There seemed not a shred of interest from any of them. I could not believe it. The wonderful healing work of spiritual healers from the Other Side had been taken for granted, not that the Spirit ever asks for thanks. But I was very disappointed indeed.

I knew there would be no further purpose served in trying to create interest in the matter for all concerned. In later years I came to realise that they, like thousands of other people, were just not ready to accept the Power of the Spirit in helping the sick. Neither were they ready to accept the existence of the Spirit regarding life after physical death. People will only accept these facts when they are ready to do so.

I shall always remember Mr. Edwards and his wife with deep affection. As they both passed to the Higher Life some years before Mother and Father, I know they were both waiting to greet them when it was their turn to be called. Without doubt, they must have had many a laugh over Freddie, the King Rat, for if it had not been for him, none of the events I have related would ever have happened.

Wobbles Eggars

ROY Eggars phoned in July 1988, to say Wobbles, his pet cat, had a leg injury. He thought she had been chased up a tree by a dog. Wobbles was unable to use her leg.

Mr. Eggars took her to the vet, who gave her two injections. He stated if she was no better, he would X-ray her leg the following week.

As I was talking to Mr. Eggars on the phone, Charlie said:"Tell Wobbles' friend to get a bowl of warm water and put in a dessertspoon of salt. Put the cat's leg in it up to the thigh as the damage is equivalent to a human cartilage in the knee. It needs attention, and is extremely painful for Wobbles."

Charlie requested Mr. Eggars should gently massage Wobbles' leg while in the water, and said he would be there to give healing.

According to Charlie's version, poor Wobbles had been accosted by a very large dog, who was full of love and good intentions towards her and just wanted a friendly little chase. But Wobbles, being a bit old in the tooth at thirteen years, was not prepared to take any chances as she had been chased before and learnt by experience. She panicked and shot up the tree like a streak of lightening, badly hurting her leg in the process. No one was more surprised than the dog.

The next day, Dawn Eggars phoned with the news. Wobbles "is much better. She is now putting her foot on the ground and sitting more comfortably."

Charlie again advised the salt water and treatment to be used, promising he would be there. Nine days came later further news: "Wobbles has steadily improved and now just limps slightly. Yesterday she climbed on the roof." A fortnight later she was fine.

Wobbles is now eighteen years old, a little old lady who is extremely alert. According to Mrs Eggars, when she is preparing a fish meal, Wobbles demands and sees that she gets her fair share. She is still enjoying her life.

Boyo

AS dear Boyo walked into the centre with Helen Henderson for contact healing, I was struck by his impeccable good manners and thought, "What a polite gentleman you are!" He was a very handsome nine-year-old German Shepherd.

Boyo had cataracts on both eyes along with eczema on his back and tail, and other parts of his body.

As we touched him, I was able to pick up his thoughts. Boyo was pleased and happy to be in the animal sanctuary; he felt it was very restful and peaceful. In fact, he liked it very much indeed! Boyo glanced at his mistress, thanking her for bringing him.

He listenend intently to Charlie talking to him, with Spot joining in from time to time. Charlie told Boyo and me that the cataracts were not advanced at the time, but he would give him healing for them, and also help with his eczema condition.

Mrs. Henderson brought Boyo several times for healing. The cataracts did not worsen, he was able to see very well and his skin cleared completely of eczema.

A few weeks ago, it was reported Boyo had maintained very good progress. The last time I saw him, he thanked us and said how much he had enjoyed his visits. He was indeed a perfect gentleman.

Jordon Till

THE following is an account written by Sue Till and printed by "Psychic News." I am very pleased it was published because it warned other pet owners of the dangers which in this day and age lurk around. Headed "Dog's healing has happy tale," the story stated:

"Animal lover M. Till sought healing help for Jordan, a four-year-old, flat coated retriever, after returning from a weekend visit to friends in Lincolnshire.

"Mike Till stated, 'When we returned on the Monday, Jordan began to act very strangely.' The pet started running around the house, whining and panting very loudly. He seemed very ill at ease and could not settle down. 'Jordan kept us awake at night with this behaviour.'

"Waiting to see if Jordan would improve during the night, the Till's were alarmed to find his condition had worsened considerably by the following morning.

"'On Tuesday,' Mr. Till recalled, 'he was very lethargic. By the afternoon he appeared to be paralysed and howled with pain when we tried to lift him up into a standing position. We contacted the vet, who agreed to see him at his surgery that evening. By that time Jordan could stand, but walked with difficulty. The vet examined him and confirmed that neither the stomach nor the prostate gland were swollen and that the anal passage was not blocked. As a precaution, the vet gave him two injections, one antibiotic and one hormone.'

"Expecting a rapid conclusion to Jordan's illness, Mr. Till again contacted the vet when the dog's condition deteriorated further still. The next day 'Jordan recommenced his previous behaviour by running and whining. By Thursday,

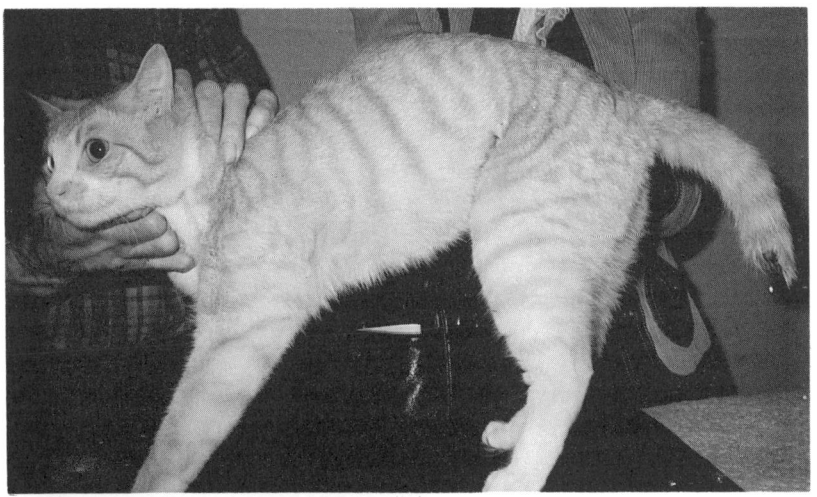

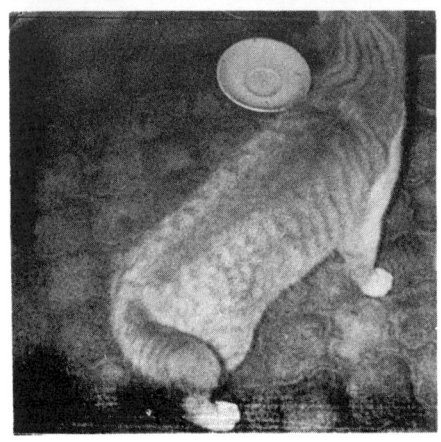

Ginger Hart was on his last legs when he came for healing, and suffered from a variety of complaints, including a paralysed tail. But after successful spirit "surgery," he made a remarkable recovery ... and ended up with a bob-tail.

"CHARLIE KEMP. SPIRIT VET."

"SPOT" - KEMP

These spirit-inspired drawings show Charlie Kemp and Spot, his beloved companion, who have helped so many animals find good health again.

Above Irene Sowter appears with Tom Gill and – to the right – with husband Gerald and Misti Barley. (Pictures by Paul Stanley).

Here Duke Owen – his vet advised having him put down – is seen before and after healing. Now this sandy-coloured dog is literally bright eyed and bushy tailed.

Here Tracey Smale is seen with Goody, her bay mare . . . and her cure was certainly no horse play. Before healing, it seemed her showing and jumping days were over. But as the picture above shows, Goody was restored to full health.

Sammy, a much-loved pet rat, really is head and shoulders above his owner Alan Martindale following a spirit "operation." (Picture by courtesy of the "Surrey Mirror.")

It's a busy life for healers Irene and Gerald Sowter, but here they snatch a quiet moment or two in the beautiful flower filled garden at their home. (Picture by Paul Stanley).

he began shaking his head furiously and banging it on the floor. He became listless once again and would not eat.

"'On Friday, we took him back to the vet, who cleaned out the ear canals and gave us ear drops and sedatives to dispense if we thought necessary.

"'On the same evening,' Mr. Till continued, 'Jordan continued to shake and bang his head. When he began vomiting, we realised something was very seriously wrong.'

"In desperation, the Till's took Jordan to the Universal Healing Centre run by Irene and Gerald Sowter. The healers agreed to see the dog at once. 'Within a minute of laying her hands on Jordan,' Mr. Till explained, 'Mrs. Sowter stated the dog was suffering from acute stomach pains and headache. Clairvoyantly, she could see poison being sprayed on the ground and the dog lapping it up.'

"'We have no poisonous substances at home,' Mr. Till stressed. 'Jordan never leaves the confines of our home without us. My wife decided to contact our friends in Lincolnshire and told them about Irene's message.

"'Most alarmed, they admitted that prior to our arrival, they had sprayed their gravel drive with a very powerful weed killer. During our stay there, they had thrown out pieces of cake on to the gravel for the birds. Jordan had lapped them up.'

"Mr. Till added: 'I thought the healing was remarkable. The following day our dog seemed quite normal, showing none of his previous symptoms. He ate well and enjoyed a long walk. Since then he has been in excellent health and has required no more healing visits.'

"Mr. Till's letter ended with, 'Our gratitude goes out to Spirit for the excellent healing we witnessed and, of course, to Mrs. Sowter for her kind attention and for being able to diagnose clairvoyantly an illness that truly had us baffled.'

"Mrs. Till later reported that her friends do not put down weed-killer any more – they were very upset – and stated they prefer the weeds now."

Behind the scenes, when we were giving healing to Jordan, I saw Spot put his front right leg across Jordan's neck and rub his head against his: it was very moving. Charlie informed me Jordan was "seriously ill" through a deadly poison, and that it was "burning through him" from top to toe. Apart from "excruciating pains, it is causing blindness. This poor animal cannot see properly. He is terribly frightened, hence the banging of his head. I do not know if I can save him to live out his life span on earth. Do not inform his owners of this as they will be upset."

As Charlie was talking to me, I suddenly saw two of his young students appear. One of them was holding an instrument rather like an injection needle. But instead of a point it was rounded at the bottom and it was filled with a blue fluid. I realised then how urgent Charlie considered the matter to be. Going into a light trance state, I placed my hands on Jordan and saw and felt a great flash of blue as Charlie placed the "injection" against Jordon's stomach. As I watched the fluid enter into him, I felt the "burning of the poison" cooling down, and became aware of peace and calm being restored to him.

Sadly, in Janury 1991, Jordon, then six years old, suddenly developed a rapidly growing external malignant cancer at the bottom of his spine and tail. As it was also spreading through his body, the vet wisely put him to sleep. I remember how concerned Charlie was when we first met Jordon and his words. Through the deadly poison, Jordon had not lived out his life span. Charlie stated the poison "was the main factor to cause the cancer." No doubt, Jordon is thoroughly enjoying his new life, completely free.

Chapter 6

What I believe

WHAT is spiritual healing and the meaning of it? To me it means communication with the Spirit. I sincerely hope by writing this chapter to lay the ghost of a question which those who sit in judgement without any knowledge whatsoever of the work of myself and others of my ilk may ask, should they truly seek the answer.

Many a time, that old hoary chestnut of a question has been put in front of me, sometimes aggressively, "Does Jesus Christ heal through you?" I always reply: "No, he does not. I have no proof at all that he does. But I am aware of the spirit healers, including a spirit vet and three spirit surgeons who do. They use the power of God's healing energies and His love, and the proof of their existence lies with their remarkable healing achievements."

Why questioners of certain religious denominations should take it upon themselves to think that spiritual healers should only give healing to those in need via Jesus Christ is beyond comprehension! I say "Good luck" to them if they wish to continue to think that Christ was the only healer allowed by God to administer healing to mankind. So be it. Obviously, they cannot see any further than their noses. This may be the cause of their extremely narrow outlook regarding the good works of others.

The Almighty goes under many different names according to ethnic origin, but all true spiritual belief is the same. Nevertheless, if those who hold rigidly cemented, biased teachings in their shuttered minds would attempt to let in a little shaft of light into other fields of healing activities, they would soon discover that God or Christ do not make specific declarations before any healer can help another. They would also find that apart from Jesus, there are literally hundreds of healers, if not thousands, residing in the world of spirit, all working through physical channels for the benefit and welfare of sick creatures on earth.

Perhaps as flawed human vessels containing spirit, many people are afraid to venture beyond the security of that with which they have been indoctrinated.

I believe the image of Christ, with its negative idolatry, should have been laid to rest centuries ago. I also believe that Christ was an extraordinary man, but with faults and failings like any human. All must have these while living within a physical body. He, I truly think, is not the only son of God as his devotees wish to believe for we are all sons and daughters of the Great Eternal Spirit, the source of all life. There are no special favourites.

Jesus Christ must have arrived in this world by the same system of production as all forms of animal life. I cannot accept a virgin birth, although recent newspaper accounts have now affirmed this is scientifically possible thanks to the meddling of man. But we speak of two thousand years ago. If Christ chose to be born the son of man, he would surely have selected the same process of birth, with all its implications. The myth has been allowed to build up through the ages (starting in the third century A.D.) by those who weave fairy tales for their own power.

Shall we take a good hard, look at Jesus Christ, to see him in the bright light of day, brush aside the cobwebs of centuries past, and look at him without rose coloured glasses and shallow tinsel trimmings and meaningless symbols?

I believe that as a man, he donned the cloak of service to mankind: he had a job to do, a spiritual mission to carry out. Christ became an outstanding shining figurehead to the world, as we all know. But we cannot cast aside the real facts to this great man's background which have been distorted by thousands of years of dogma and still is, more's the pity.

Without doubt, apart from being one of the greatest spiritual healers possessing a most extraordinary healing power ever to walk the earth plane to date, Jesus Christ was also a powerful psychic and a well-developed medium of the highest degree. He was endowed with all the gifts of the Spirit, including clairvoyance, clairaudience, transfiguration and so on.

If one digests the New Testament and reads between the lines, the true facts of Christ's spiritual and psychic capabilities are there, talking loud and clear. And if the ostriches who prefer to keep their heads buried in the sand were to glance up they would soon get the message. It is impossible to shut one's eyes to the fact that the New Testament is a book packed with recorded psychic and spiritual experiences in which Christ participated. He "saw" visions and "heard" voices. In other words, plainly speaking, he was in communication with those living in the spirit world. We cannot side step his disciples. They also were mediums and psychics. Just like other mediums of his day, before and since, Christ worked with his particular group, just like thousands of others, including spiritual healers who carry out their spiritual missions in love and dedication today.

Does Christ, I wonder, reflect with sadness that his teaching "To love one another" has become distorted, if not completely fallen apart and conveniently forgotten, especially by those who assume that only they by their belief will achieve salvation? These are the misguided ones who like to think they have gained favours from the Master and therefore will be granted sole rights to "Christ's Kingdom." What exactly is it? Such assume the rights to erect a soap box for themselves, take up picketing and form themselves into unpleasant mobs bearing the sign of the cross. Incidently, the swastika is an earlier form of the cross in reverse! With hate in their eyes and hearts, they deliberately set about publicly to harass and try to destroy the God-given spiritual good works of others who, without fear of the threatened menace, give forth help in love and peace where it is needed most.

Is the roar of the crowd any different from Christ's day? Definitely not. Look at the way he was harassed for practising his psychic and spiritual gifts. Present-day agitators would do well to take note of this for there are "None so blind as those that cannot see."

The sooner the erroneous ideology surrounding Jesus Christ – which I'm sure he did not want – is thrown out of the window and the corners swept clean, the better for in the spirit world, which is the world of reality, there is no pecking order. Fame, fortune and acclamation of the crowds are not of any importance whatsoever: clay pedestals have no place.

Looking into the life and the remarkable spiritual work of Christ, which was of such great standing and depth, I could not imagine him suffering from an outsize ego. Therefore, he would not wish to be idolised or worshipped. I believe he knew he was not God, just a part of Him, like everyone else. Through the centuries to the present day, he must be thoroughly bored and perhaps slightly amused to hear fanatics asking his healing colleagues on earth, "Does Jesus Christ heal through you?" He would probably think what a pity they cannot open their minds to receive and accept the correct answers, thereby helping them on their journeys of life.

How Christ must long for the questioners and others to get him into focus instead of gazing at him through a blurred lens, cross-eyed. However, I wonder what would happen if this wonderful man, who courageously worked in the area of psychical life, were to announce to the general public today that he had been a spiritual healer, medium and psychic. Would his worshippers still look upon him in the same fogged, blinded way as of old? Perhaps now that I have hopefully given food for thought, they will be able to see him more clearly as he really was, a superb medium who wanted to share his spiritual blessings and show the world the light of the Spirit. Judging by the outcome of his particular journey on earth at that moment of time, not many people were prepared to look and listen then: what of now?

Contrary to the beliefs of many of Christ's followers who live in hope of his return to earth, in the same form as before, I regret to say I believe it is not likely. His past role was another chapter in his many lives like thousands of others in true service to mankind, and the Eternal Spirit.

I respect and admire him for the quality of his work on this plane. Although I cannot say I am a follower kneeling in adoration at his feet, I can truthfully say my husband and myself – like many hundreds of spiritual healers – follow and tread the same pathway as he did by healing and helping those who are sick in body and mind. Like Christ, we do not interrogate them about their allegiance. It is of no consequence.

Unlike those who declare they have a direct line to Jesus Christ, I feel I appreciate this great man. In fact, I feel I know his motives very well indeed, being able to identify with certain aspects of him. Despite the proclamations of others, his wonderful methods of healing by the spiritual energies were, weighing up the pros and cons, no different from the spiritual healers of today. There is no difference at all.

There will always be spiritual leaders of great stature in this world. Christ was one of them. But he was also, like everyone else, a cog in the Universal wheel of life which forever keeps turning, old cogs constantly being replaced by the new. Some cogs are larger than others, but without even the smallest cog, the machine would stop!

For the benefit of readers, I refer here to the Church of England's investigation into Spiritualism after a committee was appointed by the Archbishops Canterbury and York. Relating to the investigation, the following article was written by A.W. Austen:

The Church of England committee, appointed in 1937 by the Archbishops to investigate Spiritualism, carefully studied the subject for two years and handed in its reports. It was expected by the committee and the general public that the guidance contained therein would be made available to the rank and file of the Church of England who, up to then, had been given no official lead whatsoever regarding communication with the dead.

When a "decent" interval had elapsed and no statement had yet been made, inquiries were instituted. It was learned that the House of Bishops had taken the surprising step of pigeon-holing the reports. For nine years the reports were kept secret. One morning there mysteriously appeared on my office desk what purported to be a typed copy of the Majority report.

I got in touch with a member of the committee whom I knew was in favour of the report being published, though he was bound by his loyalty to the Church to keep its secrets.

"I have a copy of the Majority report, and I am going to print it," I told him. "There are one or two phrases that are obscure, because of the careless typing, but I would rather print a slightly inaccurate version than none at all. However, if in the interests of truth you will read what I have and correct it where necessary, then you will be rendering a service to everyone concerned."

The purported copy was re-typed. A reporter was sent with it to the member concerned. What the reporter brought was a carefully corrected type-script, with every comma marked in, missing lines written in the margins, and complete in every detail.

The report was printed in its entirety in the "Psychic News" in 1948. With the co-operation of the Press Association, extracts from it appeared all over the world.

Still the Church preserved a stony silence. Copies of the paper containing the report were sent to all the Bishops. No comment came, except a protest from the Archbishop of Canterbury.

My printing of the report gave to the rank and file of the Church of England the guidance that had been denied them by the House of Bishops. To Christians all over the world it broke the news that a committee of influential Churchmen, examining Spiritualism on behalf of the Church and at the request of the Archbishops, had found that it was true and could be a valuable addition to the Christian ministry.

The following are the last two paragraphs of the Majority Report: "If Spiritualism, with all aberrations set aside and with every care taken to present it humbly and accurately, contains a truth, it is important to see that truth not as a new religion, but only as filling up certain gaps in our knowledge, so that where we already walked by faith, we may now have some measure of sight as well.

"It is, in our opinion, important that representatives of the Church should keep in touch with groups of intelligent persons who believe in Spiritualism."

The full text of the Majority Report submitted to the House of Bishops - "The Church of England and Spiritualism" - can be obtained from "Psychic News," 2, Tavistock Chambers, Bloomsbury Way, London, WC1A 2SE. Tel 071-405 3340.

Chapter 7

"Patients'" Cures

Nicky Melton

"PLEASE would you be kind enough to send absent healing to my mother's little Sheltie. Seven years ago I rescued darling Nicky in St. John's Wood. My mother took him and in her own words 'He is a saint!' Last summer, Mother tied him outside a shop: a child about five years old kicked and kicked Nicky. Adults stood and watched. Since then, he has become worse and worse with arthritis. Now I am told all the hair is coming off his beautiful tail. In the summer he had a blood infection and had his beautiful white bib shaved off. Nicky is about ten years old. He is my mother's child, such a darling. Please release him from pain as he can hardly walk." So stated a desperate letter from Christine Melton.

We inquired whether Nicky was receiving veterinary attention. Mrs. Melton replied: "When I wrote to you, Nicky was not under the care of the vet for his arthritis, as he had said he couldn't help him. When Nicky's hair was falling out of his tail, I insisted mother call the vet in. Apparently Nicky is moulting at the wrong time of the year. He is looking very sorry for himself."

Nicky responded to absent healing very well indeed. During the absent healing sessions I several times saw Nicky looking up at Charlie, wagging his tail, which had been restored back to its natural beauty.

A third letter from Mrs. Melton stated: "All I can tell you is that the healing Nicky has received for arthritis has turned into a miracle. He can now go up and down the stairs, something he hasn't done for six months. Mother is thrilled to bits."

It was reported afterwards that Nicky's tail was fine. It was only a matter (in Nicky's case) of nine days for the absent healing to take place.

Billy Miller

AN urgent phone call came from Beryl Miller. Her pet black and white Border Collie, Billy, a very gentle and affectionate friend, had been knocked down by a car. His ribs were broken, and there was a problem with his lungs and heart. The vet had hopes of recovery, providing Billy's lungs were clear and there were no further undetected problems.

Gerald and I linked straight away with Charlie. I watched him as he started to administer healing to Billy with a brilliant turquoise ray. As he did so, I saw a group of young spirit people – men and women who were obviously Charlie's students – holding around and very near to Billy small white rays of light. It was fascinating to watch them all at work.

After a short while, Charlie turned to me, saying: "Poor little Billy. His lungs could have caused a major problem. He has had a near miss, but will stay in your world." Then I saw Billy stand up and shake himself. The young group of students were delighted as they disappeared with Charlie. Six days afterwards, good news came from Billy's mistress. "I cannot tell you how happy I am," she said. "He seems to have made a complete recovery, which is absolutely marvellous, as we did not think he would live through the night of his accident . . ."

Jasper

THIS is an interesting case as Jasper's vet diagnosed a tumour in his neck. In September came a written request by his mistress for Jasper to be placed on absent healing. October saw a second letter, which stated: "As far as I can tell, there is no change in the size of the lump in Jasper's neck. It doesn't seem to be affecting him adversely in any way. He is a very fit and lively dog, especially considering he will be fourteen years old next week."

By November, another progress report explained: "There is no change since I last wrote. Jasper is still fit and well. The lump is no bigger." In December came, "Jasper is still fit and lively."

I had previously linked in thought with Charlie, although

I do not query his work for he knows full well what he is doing. I did ask if owing to Jasper's good general health, under the circumstances, he had rendered the tumour dormant, knowing that sometimes this does happen. Charlie replied: "No. I have my methods, all for the benefit of the animals. In due course, when the tumour is ready for lifting, I shall do so. Meantime, healing for Jasper will continue."

In January, his owner reported: "Jasper is still extremely lively and well. The lump in his neck is no bigger." Soon after we received her letter, I remember so clearly going to sleep one night and walking hand-in-hand with Gerald into the spirit world, where we entered a lovely room, brilliantly lit by a warm, pink light. Charlie was present, surrounded by the young group of students whom I had seen with him before. He turned round to greet us warmly. Holding our hands, he led us to the young people who were bending over a drawing, gently moving them aside so we could get a closer look at it. It was a drawing of Jasper's head and neck: the tumour had a dark red circle, pinpointing it. "We are going to visit Jasper," said Charlie. "It is going to be operational healing on the lump. It is time for lifting."

I do not remember leaving the pink lit room while I was still in the spirit world with Gerald. Neither do I remember going to Jasper, but I, Gerald, the students and Charlie all seemed suddenly to arrive. We were standing near Jasper, who greeted us by wagging his tail. I noticed that one of the young women had brought the drawing with her, and was studying it.

We stood back a little as Charlie produced a long white rod. To me it seemed about sixteen inches in length. Suddenly, mists of deep pink swirled around him and Jasper. As we watched, some of it filtered into the rod, which very slowly started to change colour into a deeper and deeper pink then into a light red. This in turn became dark red, the same shade as I noticed on the drawing. During this time, the students asked Charlie all sorts of questions regarding the proceedings. He patiently answered them. Then we watched Charlie as he placed the end of the rod over the tumour in Jasper's neck. What happened then? I cannot truthfully say. I haven't a clue for

I woke up – much to my dismay. But I shall not ever forget this marvellous experience.

Needless to say, I was looking forward to the next progress report on Jasper, which eventually came. In the February, his owner stated: "Since I last wrote, the lump in Jasper's neck has gone. This happened almost overnight. It seemed to turn to liquid in some way, which collected in the skin under his chin and made the skin there a dark red, as if suffused with blood. Within a few days it disappeared. The whole area now seems to be perfectly normal, with no sign of a lump."

According to the last report, "Jasper is extremely fit and well."

Chapter 8

Billy Boy

I BELIEVE all forms of animal life can communicate by thought power, if one takes the trouble to try to hold a mental conversation with them.

I remember when I was about five years old, my parents forever hopeful and with a little money to spare at that time, decided to start a little chicken farm. This consisted of three Rhode Island Red hens and a cockerel of the same breed – to match – in our backyard. I wondered how these were going to survive on cement and stone, because there was not a spot of soil, a green shoot or a blade of grass in sight, and certainly no earth for them to scratch over.

However, it did not take long for that problem to be solved. The always obliging neighbours offered vegetable peelings (whenever they had them) and scraps of food, including fish heads for my parents to boil up for the chickens. The smell was dreadful when it was cooking, but the hens seemed to enjoy the putrid mess and never left any over. To me this was a blessing. If they were lucky they had a few handfuls of corn, but not that often!

Nevertheless, it did not stop them from ferociously scratching over the stone. I used to go out and tell them it was no good working so hard because there was nothing for them to pick up to eat. Just the same, they seemed to develop a taste for the cement dust in between the stones. They would roam around all day in the yard and retire at night to roost in a wooden box, which Father had made and lined with wood shavings. I thought it looked like a huge coffin lying on its side. It made a good home though, complete with perches for the chickens. They seemed mighty pleased with it.

The cockerel, whom we christened "Billy Boy," was indeed a most handsome fellow. He knew it – and settled in very well with his little "harem."

Eventually, the time came when the hens started to lay

an egg each day. We were all thrilled because it was such a welcome, pleasant change to our daily diet to have a fresh new laid egg. Over a short period of time Mother managed to save a few so that she always had some in stock in the larder. Unfortunately, all the neighbours expected to be given eggs every day when they called. What output they expected from three little hens, I did not know. Although they were disappointed, they still handed in their peelings, etc, remarking that my parents could have more eggs to spare if they bought more hens. Well, I noticed these dropped hints were not picked up by Mother, who held the strong belief that "God helps those who help themselves!"

After a while, all the hens became broody. As they started to squabble over the same spot in their roosting place, Father made each one her own nesting box, which soon settled the arguments.

My young brother and I could not wait for the chicks to arrive. I often crept out and bent down close to the chickens to see if I could hopefully hear little chirps. What a delight it was eventually to witness the little chicks being hatched. I was struck by their determination to survive. As with all things, it really was a matter of the survival of the fittest. The weaker ones were given a helping hand by my parents to ease them out of their shells. It was a very exciting time for me. We did lose some, but out of a batch of eighteen, twelve won the battle to live. Mother happily stated we had a round dozen.

Billy Boy obviously believed in carrying out his work in threes for the hens to become broody at the same time. However, not content with that, he decided after the chicks had hatched to start crowing loudly with all his might about them. Before the happy events, he used to keep his crowing under control and would, from time to time, when the hens cackled after laying their eggs, join in. But since his family's arrival, early mornings, and night after night, he kept up his incessant noise, with only short breaks in between.

Naturally, it was not long before neighbours were knocking at our door to tell my parents what they were going to do to our cockerel if he did not shut up for he was keeping them awake at night. So it was that the few men who were fortunate enough to have jobs working night shifts were not able to sleep during the day. One very irate gentleman – previously thought to be a very placid, gentle sweet man – told my father what he would do with Billy Boy in no uncertain terms. On hearing the threats, this caused Mother to grab hold of me and my brother. She tried to put her hands over our ears, which was difficult as she had two pairs of ears to deal with and only one pair of hands. It was very funny!

Unbeknown to my parents, I overheard a conversation between them regarding Billy Boy. They were worried as to what were they going to do with him as there was bound to be further trouble from the neighbours. How right they were!

Mother always worried about having sufficient food to feed the family so before the chickens were fully grown, she paid a visit to the local butcher for instruction on how to kill a chicken properly. Thinking ahead, she had no intention of causing them any undue stress or suffering. The butcher was very kind, permitting Mother to watch his method of execution. Finally, he allowed her to kill one by the same way. Being aware of my anxiety, Mother explained to me the method used. It was, she said, simply taking the chicken by the neck for with a quick flick of the wrist it was broken, meaning instant death. I was not impressed or very pleased, thinking what an awful shock it must be for the poor creature to be catapulted out of its physical body into the spirit world so suddenly and without warning, but took comfort in the fact that no doubt when it found itself on the Other Side alive, it would not take long to pull itself together.

Even so, I was very distressed and concerned when I heard my parents talking of the possible killing of Billy Boy if he did not quieten down as they were taking into account the neighbours' dire threats, which by this time were mounting into mass hysteria. Some were talking of poisoning him. Others came forward with the suggestion that he could be suffocated, which frightened me considerably as we could not keep watch all night in the backyard.

I was desperate and worried stiff so decided to talk very firmly and very positively to Billy Boy. Thinking back in time, he really had done a grand job of work. The chicks were very pretty and growing rapidly, strong and sturdy.

If I could help it, I had no intentions of letting him be sent swiftly from this world to the next. I know all God's living creatures have a time span on the earth, but thought it most unfair that if Billy Boy did not watch it, he would be going home before his time was up! On several mornings before I left for school, I would creep out into the backyard and whisper to him: "If you don't stop crowing, there are plans ahead for my Mum to come and wring your neck because you keep upsetting the neighbours. You must shut up making the noise. If you don't, you will be dead. Oh please, pay attention Billy!" I repeated all this over and over again to him, at lunch time and at tea time, when I returned from school. I spent so much time talking to him that I was always late for school and had to run. Come to think of it, I was always running to school even when I had to leave one to go to another. My parents could not afford public transport fares in those days. I certainly had plenty of exercise in the form of "Shank's Pony."

In between running backwards and forwards, and continuing to whisper to Billy Boy of his doom to come, I asked my spirit friends to help to save him. They reassured me many times not to worry as he would be all right, and I should try to be patient. I often questioned them, asking did they realise how urgent the matter was? I now know better. Meantime, Billy Boy kept going and crowing more than ever, much to the constant worry to my parents, and ever increasing aggravation from neighbours. Frankly, I could not help but feel sorry for them. Their patience had at last run out. To be truthful, Billy Boy had become a real pain in the neck and a perfect nuisance, to say the least, but we still loved him just the same.

As he was such a large and very strong bird with a great wing span, I could not see Mother being successful in killing him. She had very small hands, and I knew he would put up a terrific fight for life. And I could not see Father carrying out the ghastly deed!

Anyway, I still continued to give warnings to Billy Boy, but they had no effect on him whatsoever. Well, the day of execution dawned. Mother had reluctantly decided to end his dreadful noise once and for all. It was going to be done after I had left for school. I crept out early in the morning and tearfully told him that when I returned from school he would be dead, we would not be able to talk any more in this life, and that he was a very silly bird as he had not listened to my warnings. Sadly I then went off to school. I thought of him all morning and was very miserable indeed. I could not concentrate on my lessons and was reprimanded several times by the teacher and told to stop day-dreaming and to wake-up. I was most indignant!

When I returned home for the mid-day break, I was overjoyed to hear Billy Boy crowing, but he certainly was not crowing so loudly. I went straight out to him into the yard and thought he looked a little crestfallen and subdued.

I knelt down beside him, asking what had happened. He put his head on one side and was obviously listening. "You haven't seen my Mum yet, have you?" I asked him. He turned around in a circle, bending his neck up and down as much as to say "Look at my neck, it has not been touched." Billy Boy kept the neck movement going for a few minutes, then stopped and came close to me for me to have a look at him. I noticed that no attempt of attack has been made on him as his feathers were immaculate as usual, for which I was very thankful. I went into the kitchen and found a note on the table from Mother to say she had been called out to my aunt to help her with a problem. There was no mention of Billy Boy. Then my spirit lady friend drew close to me and said, "We have told you not to be anxious over Billy, haven't we?" I thanked her, but was not entirely convinced for I felt the execution had only been postponed until Mother returned home. I dashed off back to school.

At tea time, there was still no sign of Mother. I was very pleased for I knew that Billy Boy would live to see the end of another day – even if I was not too sure about the morning. I went out to him and said: "Billy, you have the chance to see out this day and night. For goodness sake, make the best of it and be quiet. My Mum is out. For your own benefit, don't crow!" He looked at me, and I knew he had at last got the message. For the rest of the afternoon he did not send forth a sound. When the hens laid their eggs and cackled he did not even bother to join in, as he was prone to do. I was thrilled to bits and wondered whether my spirit friends had gagged him, or had they removed his voice box? Billy was so quiet I could not believe it.

Father came home quite late in the evening and Mother soon afterwards. As she was extremely busy getting something to eat for all of us, she had not noticed how quiet it was outside. It was not until we sat down to supper when Father said to her: "My dear, you have silenced Billy Boy then? I must say, although I was fond of him, it is so nice to have peace and quiet." Mother replied, "No I have not had the time as I had to go round to Anne as she had something she needed advice about."

Suddenly, she was struck by the unusual silence and exclaimed: "Oh dear! I wonder if Billy is all right." She rushed outside, with me behind her . . . and there he was, sitting amongst the little hens and his growing family. Mother just stood and stared at him, and said to me, "He can't be feeling very well, can he, as he is not making any noise?" I replied, "If he is not feeling very well, it is understandable for he has been living under a death threat for several days now," a remark Mother chose to ignore. She bent down and asked Billy Boy if he felt all right. It seemed to me that he looked at her with a great deal of suspicion. I was amazed by her attitude for she had every intention of wringing his neck and there she was worried about him and, in fact, appeared to be very concerned regarding his welfare!

All through that evening none of us spoke. We all felt uneasy. Mother, I know, was full of remorse – and from Billy Boy no sound whatsoever!

At about ten o'clock that night, the irate gentleman who had been so rude to father knocked at our door to express his thanks to him. He thought all was so quiet that Father had, no doubt, got rid of the cockerel, and continued to thank him for taking the action all the neighbours had wanted. He also apologised for his bad behaviour towards Father, saying he didn't know what had come over him, but lack of sleep at night and constant noise had placed him under great strain and stress. Father graciously accepted his apologies, but could not bring himself to tell the poor man that Billy Boy was still alive – very much so – obviously thinking that in due course the man would find out for himself.

While the conversation was going on, I crept out to the backyard, put my hand over my mouth and looked at Billy Boy, who got the message! I sent out thought power to him to keep his mouth shut tight and to stay on his best behaviour at all costs. He must have been aware of my thoughts for we all had a peaceful night without any disturbances.

At breakfast time next morning, Billy was the subject under discussion. My parents were astonished by his good conduct and were wondering what had happened to him. I thought it was time for me to tell them, regardless of getting a ticking off from Father. So I boldly stepped in with, "I know Billy has changed for the better, because I have been talking to him and told him if he did not stop his crowing, Mum was going to wring his neck." As they both seemed to be listening with interest, I decided to go further and informed them that I had asked my spirit friends for help for him. As I expected, my dear parents looked at each other and were obviously thinking, "There she goes again - imagining!" That time Father was not cross with me, but I knew he was very puzzled. He remarked that it did seem strange, and that something must have happened for Billy to be quiet so suddenly. Mother stated that she would postpone "The Arrangements" and would wait to see if Billy Boy's good intentions continued.

That morning, I went out to Billy Boy. As I tried to pick him up, I staggered for he was so heavy, and it was quite an effort for me to hold him. I spoke, praising him for being such a wise bird at long last. I told him that Mother had reconsidered getting rid of him, but only for the time being: one crow from him - especially at night - and that would be the end of him, so he was not to push his luck, because next time there would be no saving him!

He understood too well - for some readers, this may be hard to accept - but after that we never had any more loud crows from Billy. When he wished to communicate he used little soft noises, so quiet they could hardly be heard.

Needless to say, we were all relieved, including eventually the neighbours, who in the end were pleased that his life had been spared. Billy Boy became very well loved. The local children came to see him, and he often paid court to several neighbours who called to give him tit-bits.

During his life time, we had many batches of chicks which hatched. Strange as it may seem, we only had a few male chicks, which was just as well as one Billy Boy was enough in our farmyard, as he would attack them if they stepped into his territory so we always knew which ones were the cockerels. Father would take them to a farm if he happened to be working near one.

Gradually, my parents were able to stock up with several hens, all laying eggs. Our backyard was beginning to look like a small factory – which certainly would not be allowed with today's planning regulations! There really was not enough room for the chickens as more nesting boxes had already been added to the original three. But owing to Billy's new-found popularity, the scraps of food continued to arrive from neighbours. Having more eggs than we needed enabled Mother to give some away to those who could do with them. If Father was not working, the neighbours would do their best to pay a small sum for the eggs. It really was a case of give and take with everyone (if not bring and buy) and trying to help each other.

The first three hens we had were our favourites. We christened them Hetty, Lizzie and Nelly. They were treated as members of the family, and certainly worked overtime for us in the early days to keep us supplied with eggs and – with Billy's co-operation – future hens! Every day they were all allowed to walk into the kitchen for a few minutes to receive some morsels from Mother. Billy always led the way in and out. Each one knew its place when coming or going out of the kitchen, in single file. Behind Billy Boy would be Hetty, who was quite fiery if upset and had a temper. Behind her would be Lizzie, who could – and would – stand up to Hetty without a qualm when provoked, but preferred to mind her own business. Last, and keeping a safe distance from both of them, would be little Nelly, the smallest and very timid. She would always shy away from everyone who approached her, including Billy Boy. I have often wondered since how he succeeded for after all, Nelly was able to keep up with the supply and demand!

During the hard times when Father could not get employment (there were no easy takings from the government in those days) to obtain a meal for the family, Mother had to kill a chicken, much to our distress. It was generally the older ones who had stopped laying, and I understood they were tough to eat. I saw my mother give a chicken to more than one neighbour when they were going through rough patches in life. When we knew that a chicken was going to be dispatched, we were all miserable. In fact, on looking back, we seemed to go into mourning for the departed ones. Nobody spoke a word until it was all over.

Well, the day finally dawned when our Billy Boy was called "home." He had become a very old bird indeed as age had caught up with him. Prior to his passing, he tried gallantly for the last few weeks left to him to carry out his duties to the best of his ability. Looking at him, I don't think he was sorry to go!

I went into the yard to say "Good morning" to him as usual, and found he had collapsed and was definitely on his way out. I called Mother, who came and lifted him up into her arms. I noticed that all the hens were extremely quiet. Most of them were standing completely still, as though they knew Billy Boy was going to leave them. Normally, at that time in the morning it was hustle and bustle, with a lot of cackling going on.

I remember saying to Billy: "You are going home now. You will be able to crow to your heart's content." I knew he heard me . . . and then he was gone. Mother carried him into the kitchen and gently laid him down into an old wicker cat basket. Having been so restrained from crowing for several years, I was sure he was delighted to give voice – in no weak measure – when he arrived on the Other Side!

When the news broke out that Billy Boy had finally succumbed, neighbours and the local kids were upset. Children stopped me in the street to ask details about his funeral. Still very clear in my mind to this day, is one little boy who said to me, "Irene, it will have to be a posh funeral because it is for Billy." I kept up a running commentary on the type of cardboard coffin Father was making, and, to give credit where it was due, he did make an excellent job of it, even to the folding lid that came over the top.

Father was always a perfectionist with any job he undertook. His little cardboard boxes were beautifully made to measure for the occupants. And Billy's was no exception. I once said to Father when Hetty was placed in hers that it was such a good fit. He replied, "I wanted her to be comfortable," a remark that has always been with me through the years. By saying that, perhaps my dear Father had, after all, a vague awareness that God's creatures live on. I like to think so.

A kindly neighbour brought in a blue satin remnant which she had kept for years. Knowing of that dear woman's trials and tribulations at the time, we all appreciated her generous gesture and the sincere love she gave with it. We were deeply moved. That piece of satin was sufficient for my parents to line the whole of Billy's coffin, including the lid.

I must say he looked resplendent lying there. The light caught the satin, which seemed to throw out rays of different colours around Billy Boy. For a second I saw him as he used to be, as handsome as ever.

The children called on us to view him lying in state. I remember one group standing round Billy with a little boy saying to another: " 'E's as dead as a doornail! You can see that!" The other boy said: "Oh no 'e ain't! 'E's standing over there. Yer can see 'im." Mother exclaimed, "My God, there is another one!" referring to the little clairvoyant. They all fled from the kitchen, except him. As he was an ally I went and held his hand for I knew what he was saying was true, for I could also see Billy Boy standing there – and he wasn't crowing!

Owing to hygienic purposes, we could not keep him for long. I knew Father would have to remove him soon, much to the disappointment of the children. One little girl had evidently well thought out her questions and said to Father: "Mr. Clements, what are you going to do with Billy Boy and his coffin? He looks so lovely. You can't burn him; you can't throw him away; you can't put him in the dustbin and you can't eat him. Please put him on the shelf where we can come and see him sometimes." Father gently replied, "God does not want us to keep Billy forever." So our last respects were paid to our pet and we all said our farewells.

When I returned from school the next day Billy had gone from sight. With him going, it left us all feeling rather sad. I knew my parents would not want another cockerel, and that it would eventually mean the end of our chicken farm, which was really very over crowded with so many hens. Gradually, as they got older, Mother dispatched them, to give away. Over a period of time, the numbers dwindled . . . and so did the supply of eggs.

The era of the chicken farm was certainly a study and instructional period on the psychism of chickens for me. I was able to develop a form of mental communication with them, especially Billy.

They helped to widen my horizons at such an early stage of my psychic and spiritual development. I then came to realise that the same Life Force which makes us tick was operating through the chickens and also applies to all living matter – including plant life – on earth. The only difference is the design of each species. But we are all vibrating at various levels. Yes, it was indeed an exciting time for me.

Regarding my dear parents, the "chicken farm" left them with sad memories. Although times were very hard for them, they had become attached to the chickens. When dire necessity arose for them to be killed, I know my mother did not feel comfortable and her conscience troubled her both the day before the "execution" and after.

But looking back, at least in those days chickens were allowed the right to roam free. Admittedly ours only had a small space where they could breathe fresh air, but they did have room to move, flap their wings and stretch their legs. How very different to today's appalling conditions where their colleagues, the battery hens, are packed into cages and expected to function at all costs regardless of the suffering inflicted upon them. I can't help wondering how their keepers would react under the same cruel factory farming if the tables were turned on them. No doubt, they would certainly squawk the loudest!

Finally, we were left with three hens, the number my parents had started with. Events had turned full circle. It was the end of a chapter in our lives – even if it was not that long standing!

Tiger Bonchot-Humbert

VERY worried, Penelope Bonchot-Humbert, brought the family cat Tiger to us for contact healing. Apparently the vet's verdict was one of gloom, as Tiger appeared to be desperately ill, and had a disease which was terminal. Tiger had no appetite or energy and was very lethargic. It seemed his mouse-catching days were over.

Looking at him, I frankly did not think much of his chances of survival on earth: his coat had lost its shine and was bedraggled whilst his tail was lifeless. There was no lustre in his eyes. Tiger looked sad and dim, and had a great deal of discomfort in his stomach. "Yes, he is terminally ill," Charlie said as he examined him, with Spot doing his best to cheer up Tiger, but he seemed past caring.

Charlie asked Gerald and I to place our hands on the little sick one, which we did. As I put my hands on Tiger's stomach, I saw coming towards me a Catherine-wheel (like a firework) about three inches in diameter spinning round very quickly; it vanished into my hands, giving me a slight electrical shock. Then I became aware of a pink and blue mist hovering over and through my hands as Charlie operated on Tiger to remove the unpleasant blockage he had near the kidneys. Tiger soon fell asleep during the process.

The following week, he returned to us for a check up. Charlie mentioned then that he would like to see Tiger again for the following two weeks for healing. Each time when Mrs. Bonchot-Humbert brought Tiger in, his remarkable progress was very obvious. He was getting back to his old form. Two months later, Mrs. Bonchot-Humbert wrote: "Tiger is now thoroughly well, judging by the fact that he has regained his former hearty appetite. He also has enough energy to have the occasional fight with the cat next door!"

Tony Ortzen, former editor of "Psychic News," published an article (one of many through the years regarding our work) on Tiger's recovery. It was titled "Explain this away," and read:

"Sceptics sometimes have a field day explaining away spirit healing cures. Indeed, as with survival evidence, they invent theories more fantastic than the simple, natural laws that one individual can cure another by healing, and that the so-called dead can and do return. So it is always cheering to hear of a pet or baby receiving successful healing. After all, they can have no faith whatsoever in the treatment givn to them.

"I am sure that healers Irene and Gerald Sowter were delighted when their cure of Tiger, a former alley cat, was front page news in their local paper, the 'Surrey Mirror.'

"The vet, according to the report, said nothing could be done for the feline. As a last resort, his owners, the Bonchot-Humbert family, took Tiger to the healers.

"From then on, twelve-year-old Tiger clawed his way back to recovery. Tiger's owner Eloise, ten, said her pet 'was really on his last legs. He wouldn't even grab a bird that walked across his path.' Now Tiger is safely installed at home and has rejoined Emma, the family's other cat, and rabbits Josephine and Really Rude."

A year later, Mrs. Bonchot-Humbert wrote, "Tiger is continuing to thrive and do well." She reported, years afterwards, that "Tiger lived until the great age of nineteen years old!"

Cassius

A LADY wrote on behalf of the owners of Cassius: "The dog, a black Labrador, is eight years old, and until a few months ago was thought to be very healthy. X-rays have shown an enlarged heart. He is sick sometimes, part of the heart condition the vet says, and is being given medication for this. Please can you help him?"

As I read the letter, Charlie mentioned that apart from the heart condition Cassius had, one of his lungs was infected, which also needed attention.

I linked in thought with Charlie and felt the tremendous heat of the healing power going out to Cassius as Charlie administered to him. For a moment or two I had great difficulty in breathing. When I informed Charlie of the fact, he replied: "Do not be alarmed. What you are experiencing is the sensation of Cassius' condition. It will give you an idea of how trying life is for this poor dog. He cannot breathe properly through lack of oxygen."

I saw Charlie lift Cassius up into his arms, telling him not to be afraid. As he did so, a streak of purple light – it reminded me of forked lightening – suddenly appeared from nowhere, and vanished into Cassius who, within seconds, started to wag his tail!

Charlie looked at me, smiled, and stated, "Cassius has now improved a lot." Then he was gone with Spot. Shortly afterwards came another letter from the lady, "I am pleased to report a marked improvement in Cassius."

Nine months after Cassius first received absent healing, further news arrived that "Cassius is doing well, I am pleased to say."

For the Seekers

I often think the power of absent healing can never be underestimated, especially when healing like this takes place.

I am often asked: "How does one become a spiritual healer? What are the basic steps and requirements?" I hope the following advice will help genuine seekers to find their healing pathways.

I believe everyone has some potential as a healer, even if it is just smiling with a cheery word or two and acknowledging those who happen to cross our path during the course of our every day life: this alone is an important form of healing, as it is giving out love to another.

But there are certain people who, in the truest sense, are destined to become healers in the generally accepted meaning of the word for they are gifted with the power of healing. You either possess it or you don't: no one can put it there. This also applies to all other psychic and spiritual gifts.

To those who feel instinctively that they may be healers, my advice is to read and digest as much as possible about the subject by all means, but do not attempt to model yourself on others. We cannot become exact replicas of one other, only imitations, as there is only one blueprint to each of us - so far. Do not hide your light under a bushel.

Be absolutely sure you really feel from within that you want to become a healer, and not just because you have been told by somebody that you can be one.

After thinking about the subject and your mind is made up, I would suggest that for about three to four months you sit in quiet meditation before development of the healing gift to prepare yourself for the work that lies ahead. Then try to get into a class or circle with a good teacher for development where you can learn, with spirit guidance and counselling, how to achieve attunement and communication with those in the Higher Life. I will mention here that to be able to communicate, it is necessary to be mediumistic or a sensitive - which is an added bonus. Mediumship is not to be confused with psychism. To put it in a simple way, there is a great difference between the two.

Psychism is extra-sensory perception, often used for benefit. People declare they had a strange feeling or a hunch to buy something or act in a certain way, whereby they find they have gained for the better. Many self-made millionaires, people who run successful businesses, etc, or those who are outstanding in their chosen professions, are psychics: they act on their "hunches and impressions." But they do not communicate with those in the spirit world like mediums who do quite naturally. Everyone is psychic to a degree, some more so than others. It is a matter of development. However, it is possible to be both a psychic and a medium.

Regarding your development of the healing gift (and others), if you find progress to be slow, be patient. Work in love, truth and dedication with the Spirit. Allow, and give them, your time. There is no point working in half measures for to become a good healer means a life of commitment in service to others, giving to them unselfishly.

Always remember this: there are no instant healers (or mediums come to that) like instant coffee or mashed potato for all spiritual and psychic gifts must be channelled in the proper way and in the right direction to be used accordingly. This can take time.

When you eventually arrive at the stage of development to practise healing and spirit advisers have given you the green light to go ahead, do not think you are going to be an overnight sensation, and that you will cure everyone of all ills. Like the medical profession and various forms of complementary therapy, this is an impossibility, for many reasons, one being the negative thinking of those who need healing and how strong is their desire to get well. So always keep your feet firmly on the ground and think logically. No healer can wave a magic wand!

The patient will not receive any help at all if healers think they themselves are carrying out the healing. This line of thought creates a barrier, for when an ego steps in, the power to heal goes out. Humility is one of the greatest assets since self-glorification prevents success. Spiritual healers should always regard themselves as instruments of the Divine – and nothing more.

If working with a group or just with another healer, it is essential that love and harmony always prevail. Spiritual healers should be able to render themselves receptive to the spirit agencies who control the healing energies, the cosmic rays, thereby becoming a channel for the transmission of the healing power to the patient, who is generally aware of heat penetrating into the body.

To obtain some understanding of the science of spiritual contact healing (and I shall write more in depth about this subject and absent healing in another book at a later stage) it is necessary to point out that we do not consist of flesh and blood alone.

Regarding contact healing, the laying-on of hands (or absent/distant healing) is not just a matter of healing the physical body but healing the whole. The mind, body and spirit self must balance in harmony. If there is disharmony within, then aches, pains and illnesses can follow.

This also applies to animals and all other forms of living matter. Then there is absent or distant healing, a form of prayer healing (solely to some healers), a mental call, an SOS by spiritual healers for help for those afflicted, and who are not able to attend a healing sanctuary. On receiving requests for healing, whether it be by letter or phone, Gerald and I enter the names of those in need, including animals, on our absent healing prayer list. Every day we intercede on behalf of and benefit for the absent healing patient, and link with the power of God's love in attunement and co-operation of our spirit doctors and spirit vet. They then direct the healing energies to the patients for distance and time is no barrier to those in the spirit world. Spiritual healing is not to be confused with "faith healing," which, frankly, is a misnomer. To have faith is a great comfort when one is seriously ill, but it definitely is not a guarantee for recovery. For how does faith apply to cured atheists, babies, small children and animals?

To return to those who may become healers in due course, although I have devoted most of this short section to spiritual healing and spirit communication, it is not a necessity to be a medium or a sensitive. There are literally hundreds of healers who are completely unaware of the Spirit, but conscious of the power of healing flowing through their hands. They work in love and dedication for their fellow man. Obviously they have found the pathway which suits them best. Nevertheless, the power of God's healing energies are the same regardless of who applies them: they certainly are not allotted to just a chosen few.

Contrary to popular belief, to become a healer, it is not at all important to belong to any specific religious order . . . and that also includes Spiritualists. We must not adopt a "Holier than Thou" attitude for healing is a universal, natural, simple process which flows and flows when love – the main factor – is given out to another. God and the Spirit do not sectorise the healing fields. The same applies to all other areas of spiritual and psychic matters. No one, regardless of belief, is any more favoured than anybody else. We are all given opportunities to open our eyes, should we so wish.

Last, but not least, a lot of healers – whether they be spiritual, psychic, colour healers, or otherwise – think they can give healing only to humans. This is not so. They can administer healing to animals and other forms of life as well – and why not? The healing power is meant to be shared and used. Unless they particularly wish to do so, there is no reason at all for any healer to restrict his or her gift to man alone as he does not have the right to declare a lease or freehold on it. It is not solely his domain, I am glad to say.

George Parker

GEORGE was a very lovable little old gentleman of fourteen years troubled with arthritic legs, a growth in his stomach and, to make matters worse, was also incontinent.

I was very aware of the pain he felt through the arthritis when Mr. and Mrs. Parker brought him to us in March 1986, seeking healing help for him. I thought how very akin to the human race animals are when they become old as they develop the same complaints, but can always be put down when pain becomes unbearable. So far, this does not apply to humans, but will most probably be allowed in the future, not always for the best as there will always be those who would, if given the chance, dispose of others for their own ends.

That said, back to dear George, giving out love and harmony to those around him. Although his physical body was under "seige," his spirit self was radiant as he looked at Gerald and me.

George was able to speak with his eyes. I knew he was so

tired and weary he wanted to leave his old body and quit this world soon. He turned his head towards the sanctuary door as Charlie and Spot arrived. They moved close to him as he greeted them. Charlie spoke softly to him and said, "Old boy, your time is not up yet on earth, but I will help you to lead a more comfortable life during the space of time you have left here." George understood perfectly well, and painfully settled down to receive healing. Charlie operated on the growth which was in the intestine, and giving George a lot of discomfort.

Mrs. Parker said he had always been an extremely clean dog in the house, but was unable to stop having "accidents" indoors as he could not control his urine. Poor little fellow. I could understand his frustration. George visited us once a fortnight for healing. Progress seemed slow at first, then he started to improve. By July 1986 he had made excellent progress generally, and had literally been rejuvenated by Charlie.

Mrs. Parker informed us that George, "when passing stools in the garden, also passed black matter with them. Since then, the lump has disappeared. George is eating very well and running about. His legs are not troubling him. He is so eager to get out and about, taking a great interest in life again."

Although there was a good improvement with the incontinence, it still needed a little attention. Healing was given for this for a short time only. By August 1986, George had maintained his excellent progress, so Charlie decided to discharge him. We were all pleased, but as I looked at George I wasn't sure whether he was happy about it or not.

Quite suddenly, soon after Christmas, we received a phone call from Mrs. Parker: George's condition had deteriorated; he was listless and very tired. Could she bring him in for healing? Of course! I sent out my thoughts to Charlie, telling him George needed his help again. I heard Charlie reply to me that "His earth journey is now drawing to a close."

When Mr. and Mrs. Parker brought George in to us again, I knew by the way he glanced at me that he was very much looking forward to going into the Higher Realms of Light.

Charlie, with us, gave him healing. He did not have any pain whatsoever. Charlie spoke very softly to George, telling him that when the time came for him to leave his body, when God called him Home, he would be there with Spot by his side and would take him into the Light.

As George listened to the reassuring words, I became aware of the great relief surging through his mind. Yes, he certainly was prepared for his new life.

Charlie had a similar conversation with Mr. and Mrs. Parker. They were naturally very anxious and deeply concerned regarding their dearly loved pet, who through the years had given them such joy, love, trust and companionship.

They were put at ease as Charlie informed them not to bring George to the centre any more as he would receive absent healing until the call came, but could make him comfortable. In due course, they would find he had just slipped away out of the body.

In January 1987 came a phone call from Mrs. Parker. "George has been sleeping a lot," she said, "lying on his bed in our bedroom where he always slept. I left the bedroom for about four minutes and when I returned, dear George had slipped away so quietly . . ." Once again, Charlie had kept his promise.

As I put the phone down and turned round, I was not surprised to see George looking fit and bouncing with energy, happy and smiling, wagging his tail furiously, standing between Charlie and Spot. They stood there for a matter of seconds, then they were gone.

How George's spirit self must have soared into the world of spirit – for he had got his wish granted at last!

Here I would like to include a touching poem by Liza Hayes. It is entitled "Old Faithful."

So you can't hear my voice, but I can hear yours, and I hear your footsteps, but not you my paws. My body has left you, my heart never will, so think of me playing, not silent and still. We'll meet again soon, but you'll come to me, it won't take forever, just wait and see. Think of me often, but leave your eyes dry, I don't like to see you sad when you cry. So you can't hear my voice, and neither my bark, but I'm always around you, in light, in dark.

Chapter 9

No Card Needed

LET us look a little further into life beyond death. How many people, I wonder, stop and pause for a while during their hectic lives and actually think about where have we come from before being born on earth? We don't just happen: we are not instant beings, neither are any of God's creatures.

I believe that before our arrival on this material plane, our earth lives are planned ahead, regarding our sex, the nationality we are going to adopt, the families and the environment into which we will be born.

These plans are made in the world of the spirit. This is where we all come from in the first place and to which we all return when our number is up and God calls us "home." This is regardless of our particular religious beliefs, which we most certainly are not requested to declare. Neither - thank God - is a union card demanded at the spirit door when we are called!

For those who shout the loudest that their man-made religion is the one and only, unfortunately, when it is time for them to knock at the spirit door, much to their chagrin, they will be shocked to find they will be rubbing shoulders with every Tom, Dick and Harry from various religious beliefs. We are all travellers in Eternity. So are the animals, in their own way.

As we are spiritual beings residing in physical bodies for our allotted space of time on earth, there is no reason whatsoever as to why our spirit selves cannot travel backwards and forwards to the Other Side as often as we wish during our stay here. The same applies to animals.

Just give a thought or two to the following. How many people during ordinary conversations suddenly exclaim: "I went to sleep last night and had a most unusual dream. I seemed to be walking in a lovely park or garden when I thought I heard my dear old dog barking in the distance. I stopped to listen. Then I saw him running towards me, fit and well. He jumped up to me in greeting like he used to do before he died. It was only a dream, but it was lovely."

Literally thousands of people have similar experiences with their animals during such "dreams" and recall talking with their so-called dead relatives, friends and acquaintances of many years gone by. These experiences are not dreams, which are an entirely different form of happening. Dreams are one thing, astral travelling and spiritual visits another. Many people, often through lack of knowledge of the subject and because of man-made biased teachings of some of their religious denominations, simply do not understand that when they think they are dreaming, they are, and have been, in the spiritual company of their beloved pets and their dear ones in the Higher Spheres.

Through the years, my husband and I have had hundreds of people call on us out of sheer desperation. They "see" visions and "hear" voices in their heads. It is totally wrong to classify these people as unbalanced for they are only "seeing" and "hearing" that which comes naturally! They are potential mediums. There is an enormous difference between insanity, hallucination, and imagination, and psychism and communication with the Spirit. But it is being able to differentiate which matters.

The sooner this natural subject is investigated without prejudice by the powers that be, including established Orthodoxy, so it can be utilised by all irrespective of particular beliefs, the better for the world and mankind.

These worried and desperate people, after going through the usual channels of seeing their doctors, finally find themselves attending psychiatrists week after week. With the best of intentions, no doubt, and hoping for their patient's recovery, they arm them with an ever flowing supply of anti-depressant pills, which they certainly did not need in the first place.

Owing to their grief at losing a dearly loved relative, friend or pet some think they are becoming unbalanced after "seeing" their dogs, "hearing" them barking or notice them walking about in their homes. Others have seen and heard their cats miaowing, felt them brush against their legs, and watched a cat flap open and shut as though a cat had passed through it. Pet bird owners have heard their canaries singing, their budgies chirping and some even talking. They have watched the little swings in their bird cages swaying backwards and forwards. Some people were frightened out of their wits until we explained matters to them, that these sorts of phenomena are quite normal. All living matter has its spiritual counterpart – and the animal and bird kingdoms are no exception.

Some who visit us mourn so deeply the loss of a husband, wife or other dear ones that they find carrying on living is so very difficult. Suddenly, while fully awake during the day, they "see" and "hear" their dear ones in their homes, just for a few seconds. They hear their names being called. Sometimes they feel they are being touched by a gentle caress. I can fully accept these statements.

At one of my public clairvoyant demonstrations, amid a lot of laughter, a "departed" husband returned to tell his wife in the audience that he had "rocked" their bed during the night and moved her magazines to let her know he was present. She laughed, and confirmed these facts by saying "I wondered what was happening to my bed as it was going up and down!" When such evidence is given from the spirit world of our loved ones' continued existence, how can one doubt it?

There are many thousands of people, not only in this country but all over the world, who undergo different spiritual experiences. Owing to ignorance of the subject, they simply do not understand them. They become fearful of the unknown. Frankly, there is no need to be whatsoever.

There are people of all nationalities walking around this material world of ours endowed with many splendid psychic and spiritual abilities laying dormant. Sadly, they are completely unaware of them simply because they have not paid any attention to the old adage, "Seek and ye shall find." These folk are quite normal, down-to-earth and very practical. They are not, as informed by the medical profession, suffering from "hallucinations."

Such worried souls, unable to find the help they are seeking from those who do not understand psychic and spiritual phenomena, turn to their local religious leaders. With good grace, a full heart and brimming over with pious intent, they arm themselves with Holy water and the pre-set prayers that are called for on these most interesting occasions, and sally forth, hoping in one go to exorcise the supposed haunted premises where the natural phenomena occur. This assumes without second thought on the matter that the one on the Other Side must be extremely unpleasant and therefore needs to be put down at all costs!

Generally, these efforts are to no avail. Where success is reported, invariably the spirit communicator has become fed up and frustrated with knocking at closed doors and minds, and getting no reply, goes off to look for beneficial help elsewhere.

Frankly, if I were permanently residing in the world of spirit and wanted to communicate, I would be bored stiff and most indignant to have drops of water thrown at me and prayers of no consequence said. It is definitely not the right way to deal with spirit beings.

What is needed is a trained medium or sensitive who knows and fully understands his or her work. The recipient would sit in mental conversation with the communicators, and ask what sort of help they needed. What they require, more often than not, is just a simple message to be passed on to dear ones left behind on earth to inform them that they are not dead, but gloriously alive! Sometimes they are messages of good cheer; other times communications of help and support are relayed concerning personal matters. Occasionally a spirit being requires release, either from the obsessive and misguided love of those left behind or from the guilt associated with its own demise on the earth plane. Often they bring their pets who have passed over with them to let their relatives and friends know they are together. Sometimes, they just want to say, "Hello."

The power of communication between the two worlds is quite natural and within the laws of the universe as a whole. There is no need to fear the so-called dead. Give me a "dead 'un" any time to talk to for I always feel safe and secure when they draw close to me in love, which is more than some poor souls can say when dealing with some of the living in our evil, sick world of today.

When travelling into the world of the spirit with many children and adults, I have witnessed happy reunions with those already behind the curtain waiting to meet and greet their dear ones, who have as yet to continue and complete their earth journeys.

I have seen children and grown ups alongside me taking their present pets – of all sorts – with them to show to families and friends. What a delight it is to see visitors being especially welcomed with such joy by their old beloved pets in the spirit world, who no doubt (some people not knowing of the existence of life after death) must have thought were lost to them forever. But animals live on after transition, just the same as humans.

What a pity it is that people express fear and horror at the thought of their mums and dads, partners and friends, returning from the "Other Room." They are indeed as close as that. All they wish to do is to greet them in love and say, "I am here!" After all, I don't suppose their dear loved ones did them any harm when they lived on earth so why should they now that they reside in the Spirit? Spirit people must wonder what has happened to those they left behind when they approach them to find themselves so cold bloodedly rejected in so many cases.

Where no love exists within families, there is no desire to return from behind the curtain. The same applies to animals if they have been ill-treated and unloved by their keepers. There is no such thing as "death." The only thing that dies is our outer shell, the physical body which houses our spiritual self, the real self, during our earth journey.

Contrary to popular belief and certain dogma through the centuries, with the intent to control and frighten the masses, when we pass over, there are not any signposts pointing directions to "Upstairs" and "Downstairs."

I am amazed in this day and age that millions of people all over the world have allowed themselves to be brainwashed and conned. And it still goes on! I started thinking for myself when I was a very small child. The fairy stories put in front of me to digest did not go down with me at all well as they did not add up and or make any sense to me. I appreciate all roads lead to the same God, but we must approach Him unblinkered.

On passing over, we go into the World of Light which constantly intermingles with our world of the material. We enter the particular sphere to which we have allowed ourselves to become accustomed, or in other words, that which we have sought to achieve. As we are spiritual beings, we can then operate and vibrate on a higher dimension of life altogether, not overlooking, of course, the fact that as birds of a feather flock together on the earth plane so it is in the spirit world. So many people like to think that when we pass over, we don a beautiful halo and a marvellous pair of wings. I think this is not so. As we are in personality and character here, so we continue to be on leaving, though we do strive for perfection. The same applies to our pets.

Goody Smale

GOODY a bay mare, is the much-loved friend of young Tracey Smale. We received a letter from Mrs. P. Smale requesting help for Goody. Part of it read: "Tracey was out riding her when Goody slipped and fell on the gritty hard surface of the lane. Blood was pouring down Goody's knees."

Mrs. Smale enclosed a drawing of Goody's legs showing the damage. The right leg was the worst, with a swollen fetlock and knee. It was very swollen higher. Both knees completely were skinned.

Mrs. Smale continued: "I rang for the vet. He said that as her right leg was so swollen he couldn't do any more than tell us to bathe the wounds and put on antibiotic powder. He was pessimistic, and thought Goody could have splintered a bone as she had come a hell of a thump on that knee near the fore, and may well be permanently scarred.

"The vet also warned me that Goody could grow white hair instead of black on her knees, which will make her useless for showing. We can never show her again. Your absent healing is the only hope I have. It is a bitter blow for Tracey. It is her last year for showing and jumping in these events as she will be too old for these classes. We are right in the middle of our show season now."

Gerald and I sent out an SOS to Charlie. I became aware of him looking over my shoulder as I was reading the letter. "Yes, it is a very bad wound," he said. "Inform the lady who is seeking help to bathe Goody's knees with a mixture of glycerine - to stop a scab from forming too hard, too soon - and witchazel, to reduce the swelling and bruising. Mix both with water. Come along, we will see what we can do for Goody."

Sitting in quiet meditation, I was able to be with Charlie. I watched him in the stable as he examined Goody's injuries. Then he looked at me and asked me to place my hands on Goody's back. Charlie operated on her right knee and the rest of her leg, and also gave healing to Goody's left knee. All the time Charlie was talking softly to her, she remained perfectly still, apart from rubbing her head against his shoulders. When he had finished his work, I heard him say to her, "You are high spirited!" as he stroked her.

Turning round to me, Charlie said: "I hope Goody will not be sent out of her body. There is no need for it. Inform the little one – Tracey – who loves Goody so dearly, that before too long, she will be riding her again, and they will go on to win prizes together!" Then he was gone.

Soon afterwards, Mrs. Smale wrote again, saying: "How very well Goody is, responding to the absent healing, and Charlie's solution. Goody's trouble is that she is a highly sexed mare. When in season she is impossible. She chases the geldings. When she corners them, she vamps them!"

There is no need for me to go into a detailed description of Goody's misdemeanours, but I could not help smiling to myself for reading through Mrs. Smale's account it was obvious Goody was a naughty, liberated lady, who believed in keeping up with modern times! However, Mrs. Smale went on to say, "The vet gave Goody hormone injections to calm her down, but they only lasted a few days whereas she should only need one or two for life!" No wonder Charlie had said to Goody she was high spirited.

Further news came that "Goody has calmed down beautifully. Our life is so much better now that she can be turned out. I'm sure she is happier." In another letter, Mrs. Smale, wrote: "Within forty-eight hours of using the solution suggested by Charlie Kemp, Goody's knees had cleared up beautifully and the swelling greatly reduced. When the vet called to see her four days after I had started your treatment, he was absolutely delighted, laughing and joking, and saying, 'I'll stick my neck out; that pony is going to get completely better'."

Mrs. Smale later reported: "You were quite right (Charlie) that Tracey and Goody were going to do well. They did, at the novice British Show Pony Society (BSPS) Working Hunter Pony Indoor Show . . .

"You will be particularly interested in the two photos of Tracey jumping Goody at the BSPS Welsh Championship Show at Builth Wells. I know she had help from Spirit that day. In the final judging, Goody was placed second and has qualified for Stoneleigh . . .

"Tracey has had one superb win on Goody, something I never expected in our wildest dreams! I am going to pick up a copy of 'Horse and Hound' as we have been told our name is amongst the winners in the report of the BSPS Welsh Championship Show. Tracey rode Goody in the 13LL Working Hunter Pony Class. There were twenty-one entries. The jumping course of twelve fences in the main cattle ring was a real tester!

"Only four out of the twenty-one jumped clear . . . and our Goody was one of them! In the final, Tracey and Goody gained fourth place, with eighty-six and a half marks out of a hundred. She also received a special rosette for the best Welsh entry. Competitors came from England and Scotland. And in the National Championship she was placed third. So Goody wore three huge rosettes that day. I sent up a prayer of thanks to Charlie Kemp."

Later, we heard that the loving working partnership between Tracey and Goody continued, and they went on to win many more prizes in other competitions.

In a recent letter, Mrs. Smale added: "We shall be delighted if Goody's story is published in your book along with the photos of Tracey and Goody taken at the United Counties Agricultural Show at Carmarthen, just *six weeks* after the awful accident. Without your absent healing, I am sure this would not have been possible.

"That summer evening when Tracy walked into the yard sobbing, leading Goody with blood pouring from her broken knees, we thought the pony's show career was over. Our vet did everything medically possible, but shook his head at the sight. He gave antibiotic injection and powder. There was a hole in the middle of Goody's knee which I could put my fore-finger right into. Her leg swelled up from shoulder to hoof so that she was in awful pain.

"The vet said we could hope, but there was no guarantee she would not be permanently scarred, nor did he know if she would be fit for showing or jumping. We were told it might be several months before we would know the outcome. My great worry was whether hair would ever grow again on the deeply cut knee.

"You gave me a message from Charlie Kemp to bathe Goody's knees three times a day with the mixture. I told my vet. He said, 'It is a good old-fashioned remedy which might help, and will certainly do no harm.' I'm absolutely delighted it worked wonders. Absent healing from you and Gerald brought Goody's knees back to normal. There are no bumps or scars visible. And the hair not only grew back, but in its usual bay colour!

"I could paper the walls with the rosettes Goody has won in both jumping and showing events. You would never know anything had been wrong. Goody is now eighteen years old and living in quiet retirement."

Mrs. Smale said Goody's vet "referred to her as the 'miracle horse'." Yes indeed – thanks to Charlie.

Sammy Martindale

THE following story of Sammy's (Samantha) healing was so unusual that "Psychic News" and our local "Surrey Mirror" published her story. The "Mirror" article was as follows:

"Sammy the rat is the sort of healthy rodent the Pied Piper of Hamlyn would have been proud of. And this – her young owner Alan Martindale, aged fourteen, believes – is thanks to spiritual healer Irene Sowter. For lively little Sammy recently became so ill that the Martindale family, of South Park, Reigate, prepared for the worst.

"Sammy was in a very sorry state. She could hardly walk, was badly lopsided, and overbalanced continually. 'I noticed an enormous lump which extended from her left ear to her neck,' said Jill Martindale, Alan's Mum. Mrs. Martindale explained to Alan it would be best to have Sammy put down by the vet rather than allow her to suffer.

"'My son pleaded with me not to take her, so we considered contacting Irene Sowter as a last resort, on the understanding that if she could do nothing we would have Sammy put down. After two visits, Sammy's lump separated into two halves. Eventually both burst. Now she is back to her old self.

"'Charlie stated the cancer lump behind Sammy's left ear

was near the brain, causing her to have the effects of a stroke. It was travelling across her left shoulder from the neck. As the situation looked so hopeless, he could quite understand Sammy's vet wanting to put her down. Charlie said to Mrs Martindale he hoped it would not come to that, but he would do all he possibly could for Sammy."

I was in trance as Charlie started to operate on the lump, which seemed to be growing as we looked at it. I became very aware of a brilliant red light over my head and felt the warmth of it penetrating into my body as Charlie worked. I watched him open the growth near Sammy's brain and cut right through the middle of it, saying at the time that it was the parent growth.

I asked him why he cut it like that. He replied owing to that particular type of growth, he thought it best as he wished to divide it into two parts. The red light – a healing ray – would bring both parts to a head like an abscess. Before long he hoped they would burst open.

Sammy recovered fully. Thanks be to Charlie! Sammy went on far beyond her limited time on earth, enjoying her life to the end with no further trouble, and certainly not lopsided!

Midge Golding

MIDGE was a lovely Cocker Spaniel only eighteen months old when she arrived at the centre for spirit operational healing. She was very sick indeed.

In a letter, her owner Pat Golding stated: "I took her to see Irene after eight weeks of treatment by a vet. Midge had been suffering from diarrhoea. During the last week she had been sick and not at all well in herself. After treatment Midge, was still sick. The vet said it was a diet problem. I was sceptical about this as I had a twelve-year-old dog eating the same food.

"The spirit vet commented, 'Midge has a blockage in her intestines which I will attempt to remove.' The next day she was so much better and had no more diarrhoea. My friend and I walk our dogs together. She was amazed that Midge was once again chasing around the fields."

By contact operational healing, Charlie had restored Midge back to good health. We did not see Midge again until two years later when she was pregnant and "a little off colour." Charlie looked at her, and assured Mrs. Golding that Midge was quite healthy, just feeling a little uncomfortable as her pregnancy was advanced. When questioned by Mrs. Golding as to how many puppies would Midge have, he replied, "Seven."

A little while afterwards Mrs. Golding informed us by telephone, that Midge had given birth to nine puppies, but two had died. So Charlie was right. Of course!

God's Two Little Dachshunds

"IT must be a couple of years since I wrote to you for healing for my precious gifts from God of two little dachshunds," said Joyce Weston. "The eldest dog had several tumours. One which she still has is reduced to a very small size, which doesn't affect her in any way.

"Our little one has been paralysed four times. The last time our vet said it would not recover and would have to be put down. But God took care of his little animal and he is still with us, healthy, robust with no more visible evidence of his badly curved spine which he had for years."

I remember these little dogs very well. Mrs. Weston had previously requested absent healing for her beloved pets. When I was holding her letter, I saw the dogs being bathed in colour, one in bright yellow and the other one in royal blue. After that, I had no further contact with Mrs. Weston until her second letter (above) arrived. Obviously it appeared Charlie had been very busy behind the scenes!

Little Titch

AT the same time as my parents had their little chicken farm in our back-yard, we were lucky to be given a tiny tortoiseshell kitten. He was only about fourteen days old and had been rejected by his mother. When my father took him out of his pocket, I thought the poor little thing was already dead for he showed no interest in life whatsoever. He was very limp and his tiny head flopped about. He looked such a helpless bedraggled little creature.

Mother tucked him down the front of her dress to keep him warm while she searched for a clean rag to wrap him in. That found, she wrapped him up in it so that only his head was showing. I can still see my dear parents trying to get him to take a drop of milk diluted with water. Mother was holding the kitten while Father gently prised open the tiny mouth to put in the droplets. It seemed to me to take ages, but they persevered and managed to get some of the liquid into him.

The problem was where were we going to keep such a sick animal who could not possibly defend himself against attacks from a rat or two which might be passing through from one run to another? If we left him lying on the floor, he certainly was not mobile, would be spotted by a marauder and that would soon be the end of him. We were all horrified at the thought!

After a long discussion, it was decided that our kitten would have more chance of survival if he was kept on the top shelf in the kitchen during the day where Mother kept her few saucepans. I was to take him to bed with me every night to make sure he was constantly kept warm, which I wanted to do anyway. In doing this he would be protected from a night attack.

Father, a carpenter by trade, had managed to get a few weeks' work and was able to make our pet, whom we quickly christened "Titch," a lovely little wooden box, complete with wood shavings for him to lie upon comfortably. The shavings were changed every day for hygienic purposes. Mother saw to that. So Titch was placed on high, out of harm's way. But we were still worried for although he was taken down several times during the day to receive little droplets of milk either given to him by Mother or myself, his progress was indeed extremely slow, regardless of my thoughts sent out to spirit friends for help.

We nurtured Titch very carefully for several weeks. During that time, word got around that the Clements had a sick kitten that "will soon kick the bucket." Morbid curiosity quickly brought the local kids knocking at our door to inspect Titch and to weigh up, in no uncertain manner, the odds stacked against him by passing remarks like, "Your Dad will have to make anofer coffin Irene, but won't it be small?" To each other they said: "Oh Gawd, 'e don't 'alf look ill. It won't be wurf while Mr. Clements making one of 'is little cardboard boxes. When Titch goes, might as well put 'im down the pan and pull the plug on 'im 'e's so tiny, not two pennerth of 'im!"

None of these thoughtless remarks helped Titch or me. I used to get very cross and would threaten them that if they could not say anything nice about Titch getting better, well, then they could all stay away. The kids could see I meant what I said. They looked apprehensively at each other and started to fidget, then clustered together for a quick consultation. They all promised – there were about eight of them – that if I let them call on the kitten just to say " 'Ello" to him, they would not say anything else. I knew it would be difficult for them under the circumstances to keep to their word. Nevertheless, I used to let them in to see Titch for a few minutes only, but I would not let them take him out of his box as he was still far too weak to be handled roughly.

I really don't know which was worse, the expressions of gloom on their young Cockney faces or the words of doom they would quietly mutter under their breath.

To be truthful, I knew that Titch was still fighting for his life and was not at all sure whether he would be staying with us or going through the curtain so could not blame the kids for their misgivings.

Living as we did, if any animal – cat, dog or otherwise – became sick, its owners could not possibly afford to take it to see a vet. Therefore, their chances of recovery would have been around twenty to twenty-five per cent whereas in our affluent society of today, sick animals are extremely well looked after under veterinary care, apart from those poor creatures tortured in other hands. Now it is much easier for owners to put their hands in their pockets to pay the fees.

It was a battle of survival of the fittest regarding animals in the old days. There were cats and dogs everywhere of all sorts: some young, some middle aged and others going into old age. The latter, especially, were pitiful to see. So it was not surprising with these experiences of life for children and myself to see death waiting round the corner for some poor helpless animal. When it did take place, I was always thankful to know that its spirit had simply vacated its body and was free of pain and the misery of its earth life, a happy release indeed.

However, one evening there was a knock at our door. It was Timothy the little clairvoyant, who was also at my school. He was about ten years old. Looking furtively over his shoulder, Timothy asked if he could come in to see Titch, as he had heard that we had a very sick kitten. News of interest always went through the grapevine like an electric current. Anyone in trouble did not stand alone, one of the British virtues, sadly not quite so evident in our "I'm all right Jack" Britain of today.

Timothy whispered to me, "Don't let my Mum know I have been here to see you, not now or at any other time, because she says your street and your home isn't nice like ours, and if I come here, I might pick up bed-bugs, insects and things, and your Mum and Dad are always poor."

I was very hurt, to say the least; but glad that my parents had not overheard the conversation. But my fighting spirit quickly returned. I retorted: "Timothy you can go back and tell your horrible mum she may not have bed-bugs like us, but she has got rats in her street because I have seen them so she is no different to us or anyone else come to that! And what's more, we haven't got any money, but we have got lots of love – so there."

Not having bed-bugs was a barefaced lie if ever there was one, for every one in the district had them as bed mates. They simply had no choice. Often I would see the bites of the bugs on Timothy which showed me then that even in the lower ranks of society snobbery abounded, the same as today. All little brothers and sisters together? Not on your life.

I know we are all given opportunities to better ourselves if we desire to do so, but the methods used are often open to question. I remember thinking and looking at Timothy. Why had his mother requested him to lie about the bed-bugs? He knew that I knew he was fibbing, and both felt very uncomfortable at the time. But Timothy and I understood each other very well so it made no difference to our friendship.

Timothy's father (unlike his wife, who was determined to climb the social ladder by fair means or foul) was very nice, rather like my own father, hardworking and honest. He was fortunate to have a regular job as a mechanic at the local bus station at Kensal Green with a weekly wage of

£3.00, which was considered to be a fairly sizable sum. Compared to the meagre earnings of other men in the locality, it must have encouraged Timothy's mum even more to try to live on cloud nine.

I felt sorry for my little friend since it was not his fault. I had encountered his mother on several occasions and was not smitten by her. To me, she seemed shallow and false. Therefore, I was not surprised by her attitude to life in general. She had previously informed me and my young friends in the streets that Timothy was to be called "Timothy" not "Tim," which, unfortunately, left him open to ridicule. The mickey was often taken out of him. Unlike the rest of us, he was always well dressed. Indeed, he had quite an extensive wardrobe and always a few coins in his pockets. Needless to say, the possessing of these things did not improve his image in the eyes of my scruffy, ragged and often bare-footed young friends. Poor Timothy was never one of the gang. Being an only child did not help him much either, for his mother would not let him mix with the roughs so his visits to us always had to be very secretive.

I let Timothy in, and we walked together into the kitchen. As I went to climb onto a chair to reach for Titch on the shelf, Timothy gallantly said to me: "No, you must not do that. It is too dangerous for a lady to climb. Please let me." I was very impressed by his excellent good manners. He lifted Titch down and took him gently out of the box, kissing him. Timothy looked at me and said: "Do not worry, Irene. Titch is going to be all right because my 'dead' little girl friend, Dorothy, has just told me so." I did try very hard to be optimistic about Titch's recovery, but as I looked at him, knew he was only just holding onto a very thin thread of life. He was not mobile, despite being five weeks old. It was an effort for us to get him to take the drops of diluted milk as he was not interested in food at all.

I expressed my concern to Timothy about him, but when he reaffirmed Dorothy's relayed message, I then knew our little kitten would definitely be staying this side of the curtain with us after all. I was delighted.

Soon after Timothy's visit to us, one day after school I saw him surrounded by a group of young rough-necks, jeering and jostling him. They were chanting: "Ti-mo-thy, Ti-mo-thy. We are calling you? Where is your mummy?"

He stood his ground very well as they were doing their best to frighten him, especially one young bully who had recently moved into our street, and was endeavouring to carve out a name for himself by bullying and dominating all the local children, so far with minimal success. There he was in the middle of the affray. For his age of about eleven years old, he was quite tall, but looked half starved and probably was. He was also terribly skinny. The bones of his rib-cage showed through his torn and shabby shirt. I particularly noticed he always wore a pair of old black boots with the soles hanging half off so that as he walked, he flopped along with his toes protruding out at the front. He obviously thought that half a loaf was better then none! Everyone called him Nobby.

He had hold of Timothy by his jacket collar and was looking down into his face. I can still see even now, Timothy looking back up at him. His eyes showed no fear as the young bully tried to act the tough guy. Timothy remained very cool indeed, and I was very proud of him. I wondered how he had got himself into such a situation in the first place. It appeared he had mentioned to two of the boys previously, that he often heard his name called and also saw many "dead" people, which triggered off animosity from the group towards him.

Realising that Timothy had the courage to speak openly of his convictions, I thought he certainly deserved my support in public, come what may, and I was going to stand and stick by his side like glue! I stood back from the gang. There was in all about fourteen boys. I shouted at the top of my voice, "Get back, all of you!"

The thought of a girl half their size telling them what to do took them by surprise. One bright spark quipped, "Ere, she thinks 'e's Jesus Christ and 'e's come back." Roars of laughter came from them all, but they could see I was very angry as I started to push and elbow my way through them, quite confident in the knowledge that no way would they retaliate by hitting me because I was a girl and boys did not hit girls: it just was not the right thing to do. According to the gang's principles, to hit a girl was a cowardly deed to carry out. How times have changed!

I finally managed to get to the side of Timothy, and put my arm through his. By this time Nobby had let go of him.

The gang moved in close to us, a bit too close for my liking or comfort.

Suddenly, I became aware of spirit friends around us, telling me to stay calm and not to be afraid. I found myself saying out loud, "Timothy hears and sees dead people and so do I!" It completely took the group off guard. I felt they could handle one of us – just about – but not two! Open mouthed and looking fearful, they slowly moved back a little. Then they started to ask questions and gradually began to show interest until Nobby, feeling he was losing hold of his grip, decided to ask for proof of what we were saying was true. Then and only then, said he triumphantly, looking round at the rest, would he believe us.

Once again, a spirit voice whispered to me, "Irene, tell them about Dorothy's message to Timothy, that Titch will recover." I did so in detail. I can remember clearly the expression of utter disbelief on the faces of the group. Some looked terrified and seemed rooted to the spot. At least it quietened them down, especially Nobby, who was so frightened out of his wits, he was thinking of running away. I was able to pick up his thoughts like a radar beam!

After a few minutes had gone by, rather than lose face, he decided to take some action. He got hold of Timothy, poked him in the chest and said, " 'Ere you – dressed up in yer fancy shirt and posh shoes, yer 'ad better prove to me what Irene says is true, or I will come and give yer a black eye." Poor little Timothy: he did not deserve that. I noticed he turned quite pale and his eyes crossed as he looked at the menacing fist so close to his eyes that it almost touched them. Nobby let go of him, and swaggered and flopped around him, at the same time glancing towards his mates for support, but none was forthcoming. They were visibly losing their nerve and shifting nervously away from us.

However, there was one little fellow in the gang called Mick. We nicknamed him "The Winner." I had always been friendly with him for he would often call on us to tell us his father (who just could not control his gambling) was going to back a winner. Mick would give us the name of the horse. It really was a complete waste of time for him, because my father, even if he had had the money, was not interested in gambling. But that did not stop Mick from rushing to us with the name of a "winner."

Nevertheless, I often wondered why the "Winner's" father never, ever received the blessings of Lady Luck and the windfalls of good fortune. In fact, he was often worse off than we were. His debts were extremely high. But like Mr. McCawber, he was always waiting for something to turn up!

Little "Winner," taking his courage in both hands, bravely stepped forward. Taking my hand and Timothy's in his, he looked defiantly at Nobby and declared his allegiance to both of us by saying we had said Titch was going to get better and that was that! Other little roughnecks gathered their courage one by one and decided to support us, which resulted in the group being divided. Nobby, realising tht he had temporarily lost face in the eyes of his mates, tried to make a feeble attempt to spark off more trouble, but the boys had lost interest. They all slowly went their different ways. But as I looked at Nobby, I knew he meant to carry out his threat if given the opportunity to do so.

Before going back into my home I stood and watched Timothy walk out of sight and away from harm. As I went indoors, I could still hear Nobby threatening Timothy with a black eye if our little Titch did not recover. It was a form of blackmail, if not a cash deal, certainly a violent one. I went into the room I shared with my brother, and mentally asked my spirit friends for a speedy recovery for Titch, if possible, for without one poor Timothy would be on the receiving end of a fist.

I was very worried indeed because Timothy had not been brought up to fight, not even in self-defence. I knew if the situation did not improve I should have to stand up for him – not a happy prospect – but I would do it.

Taking into account the weak state of our kitten at that time, I did think I was asking a tall order from the spirit. But as they had passed the message through Dorothy that he would be all right, I was not so worried about that as when would he be showing signs of improvement? The Spirit do not watch a clock; their time is not ours. I just had to wait and be patient for the good results to appear. I only hoped that Nobby would do likewise – but doubted it. I could see the black eye drawing nearer as the following week passed, Titch was just the same and getting even thinner!

Then one evening, Nobby and some of his pals knocked at our door to find out about Titch's condition. He greeted me with, " 'E's gorn, ain't 'e?" I replied, "No, he is still here and alive," thinking, "If only just." Nobby looked suspiciously at me, not believing a word. With a smirk he glanced round at his friends and said, "If she's got 'im, she can show 'im to us, can't she?" They all chorused in agreement. I had no option but to let them in, praying and hoping that Titch was still with us.

I lifted him from the kitchen shelf, aware of the comparison between Nobby and Timothy regarding manners, and the fact that Nobby would never acquire them during his life time. He took one look at Titch and jeeringly stated: " 'E won't be long now. And as soon as 'e goes, I'm going to wait for Mummy's Boy." I knew who he meant, became very angry and told him if he hurt Timothy by giving him a black eye, I would not hesitate to give him one as well! Nobby sensed I would be as good as my word. In front of his mates he felt extremely uncomfortable for how could he handle a girl who was challenging him for a fight? Nobby and his mates all knew that I was aware I would be on very safe ground indeed. This was one situation where I could not help but smirk, just a little. Being a member of the female sex, I already knew how to play a "hand of cards" very well, so to speak, and to date still enjoy the privileges and courtesies that being a woman brings.

Looking a little shame-faced, Nobby (muttering dire threats under his breath) and his friends left. As they walked up the steps I could hear his raised voice giving vent to his feelings: he was hopping mad!

I placed Titch back on the shelf in the box and stood looking up at it. I decided to have a talk with him and said that he must really try to make some effort to get well as the dear spirit friends, my mum, dad and myself were all doing what we possibly could to help keep him alive; he could not lie in his box forever and must try to stand up on his feet. I turned away. Mother came into the kitchen to tell me to wash up the tea things. As I went over to the sink, I heard a very faint miaow. I thought I had imagined it and that perhaps it was wishful thinking on my part. Just the same, I glanced up at the shelf – and could not believe my eyes for there was Titch with his front paws over the box.

His little face was showing over the top – looking down at me!

I shouted out to my parents to come in quickly as Titch was trying to let us know he was going to be all right. Excitedly, I climbed up on a chair to get him down, by which time he had turned over and was lying flat on his back, his tiny limbs waving in the air. He was full of energy. None of us could believe it. We were flabbergasted to witness such a performance. Not content with that, Titch turned over and stood up on all paws, then I saw a pair of spirit hands hovering above him. From them radiated a beautiful golden light. Then I heard a spirit Cockney voice say to me "Yer little pet's 'ealing is now complete." That was all. And the hands quickly vanished.

I became aware of my father snapping his fingers in front of me, saying: "Wake up, wake up! You are standing there as though you are in a daydream. What do you think of this? Look at our Titch." Father had completely forgotten I had called him in the first place to show our kitten to him. He gently lifted him from the box and placed him on the floor whereby little Titch began to show off for all he was worth by running round us and taking little leaps into the air and purring. Mother promptly burst into tears of happiness and relief, knelt down and said a little prayer of thanks to God. I could see father was deeply moved for there were tears in his eyes too, and his lips trembled for a moment or two as he quickly regained self-control.

I was amazed to see Titch so full of energy for his only diet had been diluted milk as he could not consume food. Yet here he was bouncing with life! Mother quickly gave him a little raw fish, which he ate with relish, followed by a saucer of milk. From that evening onwards he made rapid progress. Titch started to grow whereas before his growth had been stunted. He put on weight, his fur grew and shone, and his eyes were bright. Yes, indeed the dear spirit friends had given him a remarkable healing!

The good news soon travelled around. Callers and well-wishers arrived at our door within two or three days with little tit-bits and dainty morsels for Titch. Apart from the neighbours, the local boys and girls visited, but I noticed that there was no sign of Nobby or any members of his gang. Timothy had called several times (despite his mother's warning) prior to Titch's recovery and several times since. He was overjoyed that his little friend Dorothy's message to him was accurate. She had been a class-mate of Timothy's and passed into the world of spirit with diphtheria.

One Sunday morning there was a knock at the door. Father opened it. I heard Nobby say: "Mr. Clements we 'ear yer got a wonder cat. Can we take a look at 'im?" Father allowed him in with his gang, who were all there. I noticed they were smirking, and that they did not believe the good news. I thought to myself, "You are going to get a big surprise!"

Titch was playing in the corner of the kitchen with a pink sugar mouse someone had given him. He was throwing it up in the air and catching it. As they all walked into the room, Titch stopped playing and looked up at them. I mentally said to him, "Come on, show them what you can do!" He glanced at me and, picking up my thoughts, put on an excellent show. Titch took hold of his sugar mouse, flung it in the air and caught it several times. Then he did a few acrobatics, chased his tail and ended this superb performance by running straight up the front of Nobby and clung onto his chest! Nobby could not believe what he had witnessed, and neither could the others. They were dumbfounded – and I was thrilled to bits!

Nobby took Titch off his chest, held him up in the air and laughingly said to him: "Yer done it, ain't yer? I always said yer would." Then he added to his mates in a threatening manner, "Didn't I always say 'e'd be all right?" which, after a few stunned seconds, left them with no option but to agree with him. This made me ponder how easy it is to forget unpleasant things if one wishes to do so. I was only too pleased for Timothy's eyes – neither of them – would not be blacked and subject to attack after all.

Nobby stood in wonderment, still holding Titch very carefully, studying him closely he stroked him gently. I could see Titch was using his charms to the best advantage. They were certainly having an effect on Nobby. The rest looked on in admiration. After a few minutes, Nobby turned to me and said very nicely, "It's magic, ain't it, that 'e's got better?" I replied, "No, it is not as easy as that," thinking, "I wish it were!"

Suddenly Nobby tucked our kitten under his arm and said "I've got somefink nice for yer to eat." He put his hand in his ragged trouser pocket and pulled out what looked like a small bag of sweets. I was horrified for they were gob-stoppers, which kids in those days would buy for a farthing, mainly because they used to last longer! They were ball shaped, quite large in size and bright in colour.

It was a blessing I saw them for Titch had developed a sweet tooth. If he had accepted one of those in his mouth, he could easily have choked to death. I refused point blank to let Nobby give him one, owing to reasons stated. Nobby, looking very hurt and crest-fallen, could only say: "Well, Titch ain't got to swallow it. 'E can suck it like we do."

Father could see that at any moment, the way the conversation was going, I could get into a difficult situation in no time. He stepped forward, took the gob-stopper out of Nobby's grubby hand and spoke to him nicely by saying he would see to it that Titch would have the sweet after all because he would break it into little pieces for him. Father's suggestion pleased Nobby. He thanked him, and said, "Titch knows I want 'im to 'ave the sweet." I thought it was about time he and his friends left and opened the door for them all. As they filed out, I heard Nobby say to one of the gang: " 'Ow I wish my dad was like Mr. Clements. 'E listens to yer an 'e 'elps yer."

Looking back on that episode of my life I realise now just how lonely that young boy must have been. It was probably the reason for his aggressiveness, wanting to be noticed, for by his behaviour he certainly was not loved. His father drank and was often violent towards him (we learnt later) and to other members of his family whilst his mother was not home that often.

Needless to say, the gob-stopper was not given to Titch – as his liking for sweets did not stretch to the boiled variety. I prayed that Nobby would not ask me if Titch had enjoyed it. It was a blessing that he never did.

Titch's healing really did have a tremendous effect on Nobby, for I knew he was able to accept the proof he had sought. His attitude towards Timothy had changed drama-tically overnight. He was full of good deeds towards him, offered him help and stated he would always punch someone for Timothy if they hurt him, a young "minder" no doubt. Timothy only had to call on him and he and his gang would soon sort 'em out. Nobby meant well, but Timothy and I both knew his mother would have been horrified to have had that little lot turn up on her doorstep.

However, I noticed that looking after and protecting his new found friend gave Nobby a purpose in life and a sense of pride. It had increased his standing with his gang. Dear Timothy had accepted him in all sincerity, and shown him love and friendship. They became good friends and stayed so for a considerable length of time.

I had hoped that in some way or other by talking about our spirit friends Timothy and I had helped Nobby and the others on their way to some understanding of spiritual truths.

Afterwards, Timothy and I would often have little groups of kids asking all sorts of questions, not at home, but out in the street regarding "dead" animals and people. Out of all of them, Nobby would ask the most questions. One day – and I shall never forget his questions – he said: "Irene, I keep finkin' what are we 'ere for? Where do we come from?" The last words were said very slowly and thoughtfully. They have stuck in my mind ever since. And Nobby was not referring to sex!

That child was obviously a deep thinker at his young age. I often wonder what happened to him and hope he did not decide to be a "minder" for the rest of his journey on the earth plane.

Time went on when suddenly we heard through the grapevine that Timothy's parents had done a moonlight flit. Everyone was shocked and could not believe it. The sad fact was that we all knew immediately how Timothy came to be so well dressed. My parents felt very sorry for the family. Mother stated she hoped that "Timothy's mother – poor woman – will not have to keep on running for the rest of her life" whilst Father said of Timothy's father, "For a man to give up a good job at the bus garage, he must have been in dire straits."

I missed my little friend very much. Poor Timothy: the burden of his mother was far greater than I had thought at the time. Thinking of the up-to-date popular expression, "Some mothers do have 'em," so do "Some sons have 'em!"

When Nobby heard the news, he ran round to us deeply upset, crying bitterly. All his friends were with him, some of them being very moved. I remember father holding him on his knee, trying to console him. Strange as it may seem, Titch suddenly walked across the kitchen and sat across Father's feet.

Then I became aware of my spirit friends in the room, a lady and a gentleman. They were both standing beside my father (who I am sure would have had a fit if I had informed him of the fact), looking at me.

The lady said to me: "We have spoken to Titch and told him he can help Nobby to recover from the shock of Timothy having to leave him and the district so suddenly and without any warning. Titch will know exactly what to do. We have given him his instructions, for he is a very intelligent cat. Tell your parents you think it will be a good idea to let Nobby and his friends – they cannot be separated unless they wish to be so – to visit Titch twice a week so Nobby can hold him for a few minutes. Titch will give him the love and understanding he needs. Nobby will then know he will be wanted. Your parents will agree to the arrangements." Then my friends were gone.

There was no need for me to relate in detail the spirit message to my parents. I simply suggested to them it might be a good idea to let Nobby visit us twice a week, with his friends, to see our Titch. My beloved parents both instantly agreed, so it was arranged. Nobby would visit us after school twice a week with some members of his gang. We always knew when it was time for them to call for on those days Titch would suddenly get up and scratch at the door so he could be waiting, sitting on the top of the steps for Nobby. Like all good hosts, Titch would always make sure he was at home when his guests called. He never missed either day or the time.

When Nobby arrived, he would pick Titch up in his arms and carry him down to the kitchen, followed by his friends. There they would all sit for about ten minutes, with Titch purring and being cuddled by Nobby who, after a short while of these sessions of therapy, began gradually to smile again.

Instinctively Titch always seemed to know when to call "Time is up" for he would jump down from Nobby and brush his legs around him, purring. Then he would make his way to the door. If Nobby lingered awhile, Titch would come back for him, whereby Nobby soon got the message, and rounding up his gang, prepared to leave. When he got to the door, he would again pick up Titch, and give him a hug and a kiss. One by one so did the rest of his friends. It was quite a ritual . . . and Titch loved it. Holding court suited him extremely well. Regarding Nobby, Titch indeed did a remarkable job, for his work had been well done. He carried out his "instructions" perfectly.

Nobby continued to call until he felt his need for Titch was not so great. Gradually, his visits became less frequent, but he never lost touch with him and would arrive on the odd occasion to say " 'Ello" to him. Even then our Titch would still always know beforehand for there he would be sitting, waiting. I would say to my parents, "Nobby is going to arrive shortly" – and he always did! Nobby and Titch had a strong power of telepathy between them and a wonderful affinity.

As for Master Titch Clements, the "Wonder cat," he grew into a large magnificent, handsome cat, with a most unusual tortoishell coat, the colour of deep mahogany. He had beautiful, very large green eyes. Considering his precarious start to life, he remained in extremely good health and was very fit, not due, I might add, to fine foods for he lived only on scraps and cat's meat. We had the pleasure of his company for many years until he was fifteen years old, when he passed over quite peacefully of old age. Needless to say, we missed him a lot. But thinking back all those years ago, I know we were meant to have Titch at that moment of time for not only was it another lesson for me to learn, but more so for young Nobby, the little rough-neck.

Georgie

A SAD letter arrived from Doris Mullins of Harrow, Middlesex, in January, 1988. "My budgie Georgie became stiff and lost consciousness at Christmas," she said. "Whether it was due to a large lump he has on his front, more towards his stomach, I don't know, but this is really why I would like healing for him. He is such a little chatterbox and says the Georgie Porgie rhyme all the way through, besides other things."

We placed Georgie Mullins on absent healing. Charlie stated that the lump was a very large tumour, and healing would be administered to it. The next letter in February stated: "I do believe young Georgie is benefiting. He is much more alert than he was, but still has his lump, although at times, especially first thing in the morning, it seems to have gone."

By March, more correspondence arrived: "Georgie still has his lump, but in all other respects he seems quite happy and plays with all his toys. He talks such a lot of nonsense, but appears to enjoy that." On reading that, I thought things were looking up, and the little fellow could pull through.

Further news came: "Georgie has acquired two new words, which are 'Charlie Kemp.' You see, I mention your names – and the spirit vet – when Georgie goes to bed. He is very bright and quite alert after a bad moult, and there is a distinct improvement in him. The other day his lump did not show at all, then it came back, but is gradually going."

I asked Charlie why the lump appeared to be coming and going. He replied, "It is a difficult condition." By the May, Georgie was bright and perky still. Through the rest of 1988 up to June 1990, Georgie maintained very good progress, enjoying life.

In July 1990 from Doris came the news that "the lump Georgie had is very much diminished because it almost touched the floor of his cage at times."

In 1990 and 1991 came Christmas cards from Doris and Georgie, who was "full of life – very much so!" At the time of writing in 1992, Georgie is bouncing with life.

Ben

WHEN he walked into our centre in May 1987, Ben, a lovely Golden Labrador, was having epileptic fits once a month. He looked to me thoroughly fed up with his life. However, Ben appeared to cheer up as we started to give him healing, although he made it clear he did not want to strike up a friendship with Spot, who was doing his best to be friendly towards him, but I felt he would only tolerate Spot for as long as it was necessary!

Charlie proceeded to operate on Ben's head and brain, saying to me, that if he could make an adjustment to the brain rhythms, he might be able to stop the fits. I must say that Ben was very good during the healing and he appeared to doze off; he had become very relaxed.

I watched Charlie working swiftly on Ben's brain. It was fascinating, because he stopped the right side of it working completely. For a second, Ben gave a slight twitch of his left limbs, but still remained relaxed. Charlie then placed his hand on the right side of the brain, gently pushed his thumb and first finger into the top of it and quickly made a movement round to the right. I thought for a moment he was going to lift something out.

During the operation, the left side of the brain was functioning normally. I felt great heat surging through my hands, which were resting on Ben's head, as Charlie closed the brain. Suddenly, the right side of it was in action again. When Charlie had completed the operation, I heard him say to Ben: "It's all right now boy. You can go home with your mistress."

Ben stood up – I thought he looked a little drowsy, as though he had been administered an anaesthetic – but soon recovered his composure as he left the centre with his mistress, completely ignoring Spot.

Ben returned to us for two more healing sessions, not operational. Shortly afterwards, we were informed by phone in July 1987 that his fits had ceased. Several months later, his lady owner reported that "Ben is very well. There have been no further fits."

The Riley Mice

I REMEMBER one incident very well when mother told me to take a chicken, which she had killed a few moments before, to the large Riley family. The father was more often out of work than in. But I was puzzled because every so often – rather too frequently, I thought – the family had a new addition. I had heard that a new baby had recently arrived, hence Mother's chicken.

I was not so interested in seeing the new infant as I

thought every child in that family coming off the conveyor belt, always looked the same. In fact, I was daft enough to ask Mother where they were coming from and why did not the parents buy one that looked different from the rest? I was promptly told not to ask such silly questions.

But I was given to understand quite firmly that when I gave the chicken to Mrs. Riley, on no account was I to mention to her – as I had to Mother – that I had seen the spirit form of the chicken running around. And I was to return home at once.

Frankly, I was looking forward to having a peep at two house mice as there was always plenty running around the Riley rooms. The sweet, sickly smell of mice habitation was always present. The young members of the family wanted to keep them as pets, saying that they were two special mice. One of them had an unusual dark mark over its eye. Therefore, that one was going to bring a lot of good luck to the family, including sacks of money. I failed to see the connection, but as I did not wish to destroy the look of expectancy on the boys' faces, decided to let them dream on for there was certainly not much pleasure in their young lives, and they would soon come to realise that life was not made up of Fairy Godmothers bringing good luck in their wake!

Naturally, being members of the family, the mice were named Herbie and Danny Riley. I wondered at the time where was the logic of keeping them in a cardboard box which measured about six inches in depth, width and across when there were so many other mice at large?

As I stood looking down at the poor, captured little creatures, they appeared to be almost starving; they were dreadfully thin and looked like tiny skeletons with skins on. I thought they would not have an easy life in their makeshift home and be extremely lucky if they were fed, which I very much doubted!

I was wondering how I could let them escape without anyone noticing, when I heard one of my voices say: "Tell your young friends that one of the mice is a boy and the other one is a girl, and they will have babies. As there will be many, the box is far too small to house all of them. They must be released now for their own sakes. It is cruel to keep them confined in such a small living space. They will leave their bodies, the cause being overcrowding and starvation."

I related the message to the Riley kids. Curiosity always gets the better of children so it was not long before they started to ask questions as their interest grew. Eyes agog and mouths open, they wanted to find out how did I know about Herbie and Danny? Anyway, they knew the mice could not have babies because they were two boys, so there! I was puzzled and intrigued by their statements – it did not make sense to me – for I was as green as grass in those days.

I informed the curious ones about the voices that talked to me and that was how I found out about things. Some of the boys looked uncomfortable, laughed at me and said I was barmy: others listened quietly. I knew they were more interested than they dared to show.

By this time, Mrs. Riley, hearing the commotion, came into the room to enquire why all the fuss was going on. So I told her what I had the boys. She was very shocked and stated, "Time will tell, won't it?" I hadn't a clue what she meant.

I thought it was time I took my leave, saying I hoped they would all enjoy the chicken, but also thought with all those mouths to feed – at the last count fourteen kids, plus their parents – it certainly would not go very far and some would have to go without, and like the "Bisto Kids," sniff the aroma to survive.

I reflected on the parable of Jesus, who supposedly worked a miracle by feeding five thousand people on two fishes and five loaves of bread. If anyone was needed in the Riley household then, he was for the way things were going, he could easily have become a permanent resident. I couldn't help but wonder what he would have done with one little chicken.

As I slowly made my way home pondering on this, my conversation with the Riley family and their mum, I had a feeling once again I would have to explain to my own mother for speaking up.

A few days went by when Mother announced she wanted to have a word with me. I instantly realised I was going to be in trouble and would have to account for something or other, and knew what it was going to be.

Sure enough, Mrs. Riley had called on my mother while I was at school and related in detail my conversation with her and her children. She also stated she was very concerned about me, and told Mother she thought I was a bit funny in the head. Did Mother really know what was wrong with me, as I had talked of hearing voices?

Mother was most annoyed, saying I had not listened to her warning to come straight home as she had wanted me to. I cheekily replied that as I had not given her a promise that I would not speak of my friends who came and spoke to me at times, I could not see why she should be so upset. I was promptly sent off to bed early, not only on that day, but also on the two following days as well, after school. I remember my dear spirit friends coming to me as I lay in bed feeling sorry for myself. They comforted me and said that before long, the information they had given me regarding the Riley mice would be shown to be correct.

A little time later I walked indoors and overheard Mrs. Riley talking to Mother. I heard her say: "Mrs. Clements, your girl was right about my boys' pet mice. I found a litter of them in the box this morning." I thought I had better make my presence known so I did, and the talking matter was changed. I dare not ask questions about the mice. But, I was, without doubt, left wondering where the mice, the litter, had actually come from.

In my childhood days I was a complete innocent, like many other kids in our street and locality. It was some years (I was about fourteen) before I found out the facts of life in a scrambled sort of way, not, I might add, through experience! But looking back at that moment of time, I am sure that the Riley children must have seen plenty of action owing to the continuous output on the production line by their parents, blindly following their Faith to the bitter end, regardless of how the new products, every one the same in design, was going to be watered and fed.

Compared to the Riley accommodation, we were considered to be well off. They only had two rooms. One was a kitchen of sorts, so quite a lot of the children had to sleep with their parents in the same room, the others in the kitchen, some on the floor.

The Riley kids seemed to be everywhere when it came to sleeping time. Conditions were indeed very cramped for them. Needless to say, their health was not of the best. Nevertheless, they never spoke of their adult knowledge, I daresay seeing life in the raw, so to speak, and took matters in their stride. Thinking of them brings back to my mind their remarks that they knew the mice could not have babies because they were two boys. The Riley kids certainly had much more earthly knowledge than I could ever have understood at the time.

The next we knew was that the Riley mice were all going to be got rid of by drowning at the hands of Mr. Riley. Some of his children ran round to me as they wanted me to save their pets.

I thought the drowning was a bit harsh and didn't see the necessity for it. I could not see why they should not be turned loose especially as the Riley home was running alive with hundreds of skinny little mice who seemed to be forever hopeful in picking up a crumb or two, so a few extra mice set free would not, in my estimation, have made the slightest difference, and said so.

My parents had been quietly listening to the conversation between me and the kids. I was planning how I could leave and go back with them to the Riley home as I felt strongly I should try to save the pets from the terrible fate that awaited them. Yes indeed, I *was* going to answer the clarion call for help, and beginning to feel very important. I put my coat on and got as far as the door, with the kids following me.

I could not believe my good luck for I had not asked either of my parent's permission to leave home when suddenly I felt Father's hand on my shoulder. I heard him say to me, "And where do you think you are going, my girl?" I was taken by complete surprise and was momentarily lost for words. Thinking I had got this far, I was not going to give up easily. So I defiantly announced that I was going back with the Riley boys to save their mice for them. That did it! Father became very angry, saying to me: "What Mr. Riley does with the mice is his business, not yours. You are definitely not going round there to interfere with his arrangements." The Riley kids, about six of them, all burst into tears. I was sent to my room, and there I was to stay until the morning. And I knew Father meant what he said.

I was very distressed. Not only had I been cut down to size, but was very worried about the Riley mice. I sat and thought of my spirit friends and sent out an urgent SOS for the mice to be saved. I did not get any response from the friends so resigned myself to the fact that Mr. Riley would no doubt carry out the foul deed. I tried to put it out of my mind, picking up one of my school exercise books to look at.

After a while I heard a voice whisper to me so softly: "Do not worry, Little One. The Riley mice will be all right." That was all. The words came without warning and so quickly I thought for a moment or two that I had imagined them, but I knew I had not.

Quite late that evening there was a knock at the door. Father opened it. I could hear excited children's voices and knew it was the Rileys. I remember thinking how brave they were to return under the circumstances, above all, having to face Father. One of the little lads asked him if he could show me something. Father very reluctantly agreed, and called me down, at the same time telling me not to think I would be allowed to stay downstairs for the rest of the evening as I was to return to my room afterwards.

I made my way along our dark passage to the door where the kids were standing all crowded together, all talking at the same time, trying to tell me the good news that Herbie and Danny had escaped (they still called them by the same names), taking their family with them.

It appeared that one of the boys had noticed that their pets had disappeared from the kitchen. Going in search of them, fearing the worst, he crept into the room where his parents were resting and saw the mouse box on the floor in a corner. He picked it up. There was a large hole in it . . . and no sign of the mice.

Knowing better than to wake up his parents, he had to wait until they returned to the conscious state when he asked his father what had happened. Apparently, Mr. Riley had gone to pick up the box to put the mice to death when he noticed they had managed to escape.

The kids rushed round to show me the evidence by putting the box in front of me. They were laughing and happy to know their pets were safe somewhere. As the little creatures were psychic, they obviously had acted on their instincts to beat it while they had the chance!

I looked at my father's face and felt sure that he also was pleased to know the mice had got away, although he would never have said so. I knew my plea for help had been answered so mentally sent out a thought of thanks to my friends.

As the children were leaving, one of them stopped and called out to me, "Yer asked for 'elp for our 'erbie and Danny from yer secret friends, didn't yer?" Since my father was standing right behind me, I decided not to openly agree, but just nodded my head slightly as I did not see the need for an extended sentence. So I returned to my room to carry out the one already given me.

I heard later that all the members of the Riley family were called together to hear a short briefing by their father on the dangers and stupidity of catching and keeping wild animals in one's home. I was given to understand that at the time Mr. Riley was very inebriated – drinking was his other main pastime – and it seemed obvious to him that Herbie and Danny had taken on gigantic proportions. His kids were laughing their heads off at what he had said. I must admit I was tickled pink.

On second thoughts, thinking of Mr Riley now, unbeknown to him at the time, he apparently had the gift of looking into the future. When he lectured his children on the iniquity of keeping wild animals in captivity, no doubt he must have had a glimpse of things to come in our present day.

I think back to Charlie Kemp's conversation with me in 1966. His predictions regarding "manufactured monsters" living on the earth plane were so accurate. By the 1980s, articles appeared in the national press concerning the fact "that scientists, by gigantic engineering, now have the sickening ability to manufacture 'designer creatures,' one aspect being, of all things, mice as large as cats and dogs." According to the national press, through the years, some of the monsters have already arrived. The "manufacturers" have gone mad, not realising in their eagerness to change the face of the Universe and its inhabitants and trying to play God, that in due course they will let loose on the world such "creature" catastrophies! Even with the best of intentions, accidents will always happen. Unfortunately and terrifyingly, so will the horrors.

It will not be hard or difficult to imagine mice of gigantic proportions, who have managed to escape and multiply at a much faster rate than their tiny ancestors, roaming the world in droves. There will always be those at the ready to trade in a new line of business – especially novelties – regardless of the outcome.

Yes, man-distorted gigantic animals, of different shapes, sizes and manufactured to order, will be produced like cars off assembly lines. Like thousands of household pets already being ill treated, not wanted or loved, the "designer creatures" will be cast out to fend for themselves when the novelty of "Keeping up with the Jones's" has worn off.

And the manufacturers' excuse for their madness? "Designer creatures" are being developed to provide researchers with animals on which to test new treatments. In other words, the drug industry must be kept going at all costs, regardless of the appalling suffering inflicted on these particular animals and otherwise. But will it stop there? I cannot help but wonder what other monster plans the manufacturers have in their pipe lines. I would not be at all surprised if in time, animals are fitted with human brains and human voices. The only problem is this: what nationality will they be, and which languages will they speak?

Regarding the "manufacturers," one can only pray, "Father forgive them, for they know not what they do." And Mr. Riley? He was indeed certainly born before his time. Now this particular story must end, leaving readers to ponder for themselves.

Ginger Hart

GINGER was without doubt on his last legs when Mr. and Mrs. Hart brought him to us for healing. The diagnosis and advice from his vet were indeed grim as Ginger's injuries, inflicted by a car road accident, were very serious. He had a blockage of the bowel; was unable to pass stools; severe internal bleeding; swelling of his back and back legs, caused by sacs (including a large one) filled with fluid; partial paralysis of back legs; and a completely paralysed tail. This hung down and dragged on the floor. Ginger was vomiting, and not interested in food. He *was* a poor little soul.

Understandably, the vet's advice to the Harts was to have him put down, but they decided otherwise – fortunately for Ginger. As Paula Hart carried him into our Pet's Corner, I watched Charlie with Spot by his side walk in with them. As she gently laid Ginger on the table, Spot jumped onto it to comfort him. By the look on Ginger's face, I knew he was pleased to see him.

Charlie said to me: "This little one's body is slowly ceasing to work. It is badly injured, and very painful. I will help him as much as I can, but at this stage we can only hope he will recover. Are you both ready?" Gerald and I placed our hands on Ginger, who by this time had closed his eyes and was perfectly still. I noticed that Spot had placed his paw on Ginger's head. By operational healing, Charlie administered to all of Ginger's injuries. I saw him stop the internal bleeding.

After Charlie had finished and I returned from the trance state, we noticed that Ginger's tail had changed in shape. From the tip, about five inches of it had narrowed. His legs were not so swollen whilst the sacs were smaller in size. Ginger certainly looked a lot brighter. His lovely coat of ginger and white was healthier in appearance.

Charlie remarked to the Harts, as their pet received operational healing, to be patient and wait for the results: he would continue with absent healing for him, and wanted Ginger to return to the centre for further contact healing.

Within two days we received a letter from Mrs. Hart, stating: "I am writing to tell you that Ginger is doing well. After we saw you, when we were on our way to Suffolk, we noticed Ginger was wet. He was losing fluid from those sacs on his 'beam end.' Since then, he has had a more or less continual damp patch there. Ginger had to have enemas to help him pass running motions, but the following is the result of Charlie Kemp's work. This morning, after sleeping all day yesterday, Ginger passed a motion, the first solid one since his accident. Last night, my husband tickled him at the base of his tail and he wriggled so he can't be as numb as he was. His tail is still limp, but we are sure now Ginger will recover 100 per cent.

"By the way, I saw a bright light in our bedroom last night, and it wasn't the electric one. It was just below the ceiling by the wall. Ginger was on my bed purring so it must have been Charlie Kemp."

In a further letter in September 1985, Mrs. Hart wrote: "Ginger is still progressing. Feeling must have returned to his back passage as he always knows when he wants to use his dirt tray and seems to be getting more control than he had. The fluid has almost gone now. He still has one or two cuts on his tail. His appetite has increased since he saw you. In fact, the very night we got back home, he ate the other cat's food before we realised what he was doing. He was sick, but that was because he had been so greedy!

"He has been walking all round the garden. I'm sure Charlie Kemp does come as Ginger purrs for no apparent reason. We haven't taken him back to the vet as we don't want his tail off."

Mr. and Mrs. Hart brought Ginger again later that month when Charlie again operated on Ginger's tail. He was pleased with Ginger's overall good progress, but informed the Harts that Ginger would lose part of his tail as it was permanently paralysed a few inches upwards from the tip, and would be more of a hindrance than a benefit to him. They were not to be surprised when in two day's time the useless part fell off. The rest of Ginger's tail was now in action and the finished job would look nice, like a bob-tail. Ginger had made a very good recovery.

Two days after their visit, we received a phone call from Mrs. Hart to say "something" was happening to Ginger's tail. It had started to move at the bottom until the bone was showing through – and then the damaged part simply fell off! Through it all, Ginger showed no signs of distress or pain, but seemed to be more interested in the procedure.

Shortly afterwards, Mr. and Mrs. Hart brought Ginger to the centre again – and he had indeed lost the bottom part of his tail! A little more healing was given to it by Charlie, who stated there would be no further need for Ginger to return, so discharged him.

It was not long before Mrs. Hart sent us a photograph of the result . . . and I must say Charlie had made a grand job of Ginger's tail. In fact, on second thoughts it was a "designer label" bob-tail! To date, Ginger Hart is still enjoying the good life, thanks be to Charlie.

Pickles

PICKLES, a Jack Russell, became paralysed after an injection for distemper and hardpad. She could not stand at all on her back legs. This happened about three years before her owner brought her to us.

But as we touched her, although she was a lovely, chirpy little dog with a cute personality, I could feel the frustration owing to her paralysis. I hoped Charlie would be able to help her. He did, by operating on her lower spine and legs, whereby she was soon running around normally, without any signs of paralysis whatsoever. Pickles only visited our centre twice. Information given to us two years later was that Pickles had maintained her excellent progress.

Benny

ANOTHER lady wrote to ask "for your help for my dog, Benny. I am truly desperate, and ill with worry. He has always been a healthy dog, according to his vet. I noticed a lump under Benny's neck on the left hand side. He has developed a nasty raw patch above his right ear. Benny is quite unconcerned except when I burst out crying, when he tries to give me one of his biscuits!"

Later she wrote: "The patch on top of Benny's head is definitely better. The weepy, sore place has healed completely. The scab has fallen away and the skin looks pink and healthy. The hair will take some time to grow, but already a few hairs are beginning to show on the bald patch. I thought the lump on his neck looked much smaller. In fact, it almost seemed to have gone. Next morning it was still there, but not so large as previously. I will not lose hope!"

Since this communication, Benny has had an operation on his salivary gland for the removal of a growth by his vet.

An extract from the next letter by Benny's owner reads: "When I brought him home, I honestly didn't think he would last the night. His breathing was shallow, his jaws firmly clamped together, and he was so covered in blood. I stayed up with him until 1.00 am. I came downstairs the next morning expecting the poor little chap to be worse, or even dead. I was amazed – he rushed towards me and then demanded some food. His appetite was excellent. Since then, Benny's progress has been fantastic. His stitches were due to come out either on or after June 5. I took him to the vets on June 2 . . . and such was the healing in the horrific neck wound that the vet removed the stitches there and then. Benny's vitality, exuberance and sheer joy of living are a constant source of amazement to me. Please continue with your wonderful help. Without it I doubt if he would have made it."

I felt sure that again, Charlie was happy to be of assistance.

Fluffy Bradley

ANNE BRADLEY wrote to us requesting absent healing for her 17-year-old cat after his vet diagnosed a malignant growth on the elbow joint of his right front leg. Six years previously this leg was accidentally caught in a rat trap on the poultry farm next door. There was little sign of damage at the time, but it must have left a weakness. The vet said he could control the tumour with steroids, but it was growing alarmingly. Fluffy was not eating and had lost a lot of weight.

He was placed on absent healing, but Charlie was not at all hopeful regarding Fluffy's recovery and, he said, neither was the vet. Charlie would still continue with healing for the sick one.

When situations like this arise, it is not a healer's right to state to people the possibility of their pets – when seriously ill – passing to the Higher Life.

A second letter arrived seven days after the first: "Fluffy vomited dark brown liquid and white matter – possibly a growth?" I could only write back to say to Miss Bradley that absent healing was still continuing for her cat.

Charlie previously informed me that he was able to stop the pain of the cancer, but it was rapidly spreading through Fluffy's body. It was not the cancer Fluffy was bringing up, but white matter connected with it. Charlie added he was going to pass over very soon.

The third letter, received a week later, stated: "To our surprise, Fluffy began to eat again. This would confirm that the white solid he vomited was a growth."

We did not receive any more correspondence from Miss Bradley. Charlie simply stated, "The little one arrived safely . . ."

Chapter 10

With All God's Creatures

AS a child, I was given the chance to have a holiday in a little village in Wiltshire. It came through a charitable trust, the Country Holiday Fund, for poor children, via the school.

I was very fortunate to be one of the number chosen, and thrilled at the thought of going to the country with the added blessing of being allowed to stay for fourteen days – sheer bliss! And, as events turned out, it was a holiday I shall never forget.

The spiritual experiences that took place then are as alive and fresh in my memory today as they were all those years ago.

We had a very pleasant train journey from London and were supplied on the way with delicious currant buns, home made lemonade and an apple, which made the travelling even better!

I remember being met on our arrival and taken to a comfortable house in the village. I liked the atmosphere there. The husband, wife and their children were very nice, soon making me feel I was one of the family. I knew my holiday with them was going to be a very happy one.

The London children and myself quickly made many young friends, who eagerly took us around to show us the delights of the country. Their efforts were much appreciated by us, as our backgrounds consisted of tenement houses and concrete backyards, without a blade of grass to be seen anywhere.

Looking back, I consider myself to be extremely lucky. It was more than a great privilege to be befriended by a little boy, whose name was Billy. I thought him a little plump for his age. Though he was a little older than me, I shall never forget him. I certainly liked him a lot. He became my very special friend. Now I will state the reasons why.

As Billy stepped out of the group of friends to greet me, there was an instant affinity between us. I felt I had known him for a very long time, the kind of affinity that develops with someone during a past life or lives. I knew him, and he knew me.

After we had all been introduced to each other, Billy said to me: "Please come with me Irene, because I want to show you my secret places. There are many things I can show you, which I know you will enjoy and like."

I was only too pleased to hold his hand. Although he was a young boy, he seemed to tower above all of us, not physically. I was intrigued by him and gladly allowed him to lead me away from the others, knowing within myself that I would not come to any harm.

As we walked along the country lanes, the hedgerows were bursting with life, some seen, others not. I listened intently to Billy talking to me. He was saying that what he was going to show me was very special. He did not want his other friends present because they would not understand, and only laugh at him.

I knew then that Billy was like me. As my dear mum would have said, "Oh dear, there's another one!" Billy led me into the most beautiful woods which had such a splendid variety of trees and woodland plants that I had ever seen. We eventually came to a large pond. I became aware of the stillness of the pond and the quietness of the woods, apart from the bird song.

I could understand why Billy wanted to take me there for it was like heaven. I could have stayed there for ever. But there were far greater things in store to come for me. Billy let go of my hand and whispered to me, "Irene, stand still and do not move, but watch."

He stood with his eyes closed, not moving at all. After a few minutes (it seemed a long time to me), I suddenly noticed a large, beautifully coloured flying insect. I had never seen anything like it before. It hovered over Billy, and then settled down on his right shoulder. After two or three minutes, more of them, just as lovely, arrived and settled on him. Billy still had his eyes shut.

I was on the point of asking him where were they coming from and did he know they were there – I realised afterwards what a silly question it would have been to ask – when I heard a spirit voice advising me to be quiet, not to speak, only watch.

As I did so, a swarm of the same species flew close to Billy and settled on him, some on his head, face and all over the rest of his body. He was covered in a blanket of colours of different hues.

During all this activity, Billy had not moved an inch. I lost count of the beautiful creatures which appeared to fly to him from nowhere, and could not understand, once they alighted, how they all managed to stay so still.

Billy suddenly opened his eyes. My curiosity got the better of me, so I asked him what they were. "They are my friends," he replied, "the dragonflies."

Then they moved into action and formed a huge cloud of brilliant colours by flying up and down in front and around him, their bodies and wings shining, such a mass of colours intermingling. I was enthralled by the wonderful display, could not believe what I was witnessing and was spellbound by their beauty. They seemed to be dancing all in perfect harmony for Billy.

I said to him: "Where do they come from? I did not see one dragonfly when we came here." He replied, "Irene, you have not got your eyes open, for if you look for them, you will find them, like I have done."

I did not see the point in telling him that these beautiful friends of his would not exist, and even if they did, wouldn't be very happy in the environment where I lived.

Billy continued talking to me. I could hardly see his face and body through the blaze of glorious colours still moving in front of him. "I talk to them, Irene," he said. "They do not always come when I would like them to, but most times they do." I replied, "I think you are very clever, Billy, getting them to fly to you and stay on you like that, and getting them to dance as well."

Billy gave me a loving look, smiled and replied: "No Irene, it is not a matter of being clever. It is simply that I have got to know them and they are aware I will not hurt them. They dance because they know I love them."

I would just like to mention that a little while ago very good friends of ours offered Gerald and myself the chance to spend a weekend in their lovely home while they were away. It is a beautiful place with a large, lovely garden, very isolated, with ideal surroundings for meditation.

Gillian, one of the friends, happened to mention to me

that there were dragonflies at the bottom of next door's garden, in which there was a pond. Memories of Billy's dragonflies came flooding back to me. I thought: "Now is my chance! Perhaps, with luck, I may be able to persuade Gillian's dragonflies to come to me and dance as Billy's friends did for him."

I stood at the bottom of the garden, facing the one next door, with my dear husband for some considerable time, quite still and with my eyes closed, sending out my thoughts, like a radar beam to the dragonflies, which I hoped would be many in number.

Nothing happened. Needless to say, I was very disappointed. When our friends returned, I related to Gillian how I had tried to find the dragonflies, when she calmly announced she had only ever seen two!

We had a jolly good laugh. I said I did not know what her neighbour might have thought if she had seen me standing so near to her garden, not moving for some time. Perhaps she assumed I had "died" standing or that I might have been a little bit "touched," hearing me talking out loud, asking the dragonflies where they were! I wish I had the great power of affinity that Billy had with all of God's living creatures. I did not make any headway with the two dragonflies which Gillian had seen, let alone a swarm of them. But it made me realise more than ever how lucky I was to have seen Billy in action, so to speak, a chance of a lifetime.

To continue my story, Billy said: "Irene, keep still and wait a moment. Then put out your hand." He shut his eyes again and held his hand out. After a few seconds, one of the dragonflies stopped dancing and descended onto Billy's hand. Then I felt a slight movement as it flew onto the palm of mine.

My eyes almost popped out of my head. I could not believe it! I can still see that beautiful dragonfly slowly moving its wings. As I looked at the intricate delicate design of them, I was overjoyed. It gave me such great pleasure just to hold it.

I wanted to know how and why the dragonfly came to me. Billy stated so simply, "Well, Irene I told them that as I have a special visitor for a while, I would like one of them, if possible, to settle on your hand." I was lost for words!

I suddenly became aware of my spirit friends, men and women, around us, and others close to Billy. I had never seen them before. One man said, "These dragonflies must go now as they have their own lives to lead." Gradually, they all moved out of the pattern of the dance. I watched them leaving for their own separate pathways until they were out of sight.

My own dragonfly hovered off my hand, then he was up and away. I stood for a few moments wondering if I had dreamt the whole lovely experience.

"Did I fall asleep?" I asked Billy, knowing that I had not, but I wanted to make sure. "No, you were wide awake," he replied. "I told you I would show you my secrets, didn't I? The dragonflies are one of them. I am very happy they danced for you in greeting."

I was so pleased I threw my arms around him, boldly kissing him on the face. Poor Billy was so embarrassed and said, "Oh Irene it's a bit early, isn't it?" We had a laugh! But I did tell him how much I appreciated him confiding in me regarding his special secrets.

However, I was very curious to know how he talked to the dragonflies because he had not spoken out loud to them. "I just stand quietly and talk to them with my mind," he said. Then I knew I had a colleague in Billy. For he was able to communicate by psychic thought power with all creatures of nature as I could with animals.

I asked him if he saw and heard people who had "died." Billy looked straight at me and said: "Yes. I always have done. And so do you!" I agreed.

We sat together by the pond and talked for a long time, relating our spiritual experiences to each other. I was elated and very uplifted just talking to him and felt I could stay with him forever, but knew it was utterly impossible!

Suddenly Billy said to me: "Irene, I *knew* you were coming here to meet me. You look exactly as I have seen you. I recognised you immediately when you arrived."

I asked him how was he so sure it was me he was going to meet. Billy stated that about three weeks before my holiday, while he was in the sleep state one night, he visited the spirit world to meet some of his friends, when a lady called him. She was, he said, standing with a group of people and children – and I was one of them. She introduced me to him, saying that I was Irene, lived in London and it was planned that he teach me to learn about many things – spiritually and psychically – as it was necessary at that stage of my development and life to be given the opportunity to discover the depths of communication with other forms of life on earth during my stay in Wiltshire.

Then, said Billy, he woke up. His visit was so very vivid he could remember everything that had happened in detail. He also mentioned that he had noticed I was holding a little white very curly haired dog. I knew Billy was telling the truth – he had seen my beloved Soapsuds with me in the spirit world, a fact he could not have known when in the conscious state.

To be truthful, I had no recollection whatsoever of being with Billy, Soapsuds, the spirit people or of the children at that moment of time in the Higher Life. However, the mention of Soapsuds convinced me that my spirit self must have been there.

Nevertheless, I could accept all that Billy had related to me for spiritual visits and experiences between the two worlds take place quite naturally.

On my first day with Billy in the woods, our time passed by very quickly, and we had to go back to tea. I was very reluctant to leave him. Billy promised me that the next day he would show me more events of interest.

Needless to say, the following morning I was up and about very early and eager to go back into the woods with my dear friend. We met in the village and made our way to the pond and quietly sat together. I noticed Billy had shut his eyes. Everything was so still and very peaceful.

I felt that I was in an entirely different world. Although I could not see anything unusual taking place then, I was aware of the perfect harmony that abounded in the woods. To me it became a mystical place of outstanding beauty. Once again, I felt the power of tremendous spiritual upliftment.

Billy whispered to me: "Do not move Irene, or make a sound. My friends are coming to see you. I have told them you can be trusted and you would like to greet them all in love."

I heard the birds calling suddenly in a loud crescendo to each other. As I watched, little groups of them, of different varieties and colours, flew down from the trees onto Billy.

Some perched on his shoulders, others tucked themselves down by his sides. Quite a few were sitting in his lap. He was allowed to stroke them. There were quite a number, all gently fluttering around, trying to find a comfortable place on him to settle.

The loud calling to each other had ceased. It seemed to me they were talking, and some were singing gloriously, to Billy, who still had his eyes shut.

I was absolutely fascinated and deeply moved by the wondrous sight and began to think that perhaps I could do the same with the London sparrows when I returned home! Suddenly, I was startled for a large brown barn owl glided swiftly and silently past me and perched on Billy's feet.

I expected all the birds to disappear quickly at the arrival of this predator, but no, they stayed as settled as before. Several birds were already hovering over me, and I knew I was the subject of discussion. I would dearly have loved them to nestle on me, but it was not to be.

By this time rabbits, red squirrels, mice, and many other woodland creatures, including wood pigeons and several species of water fowl, had made their way to the happy gathering and clustered around Billy as closely as they could.

I felt as though I was outside a window, looking in. But I was able to absorb details of everything present and all the happenings taking place in the wood. All these lovely creatures were thoroughly enjoying the occasion, which seemed to me to be like a celebration party, as I looked at the many woodland animals which had gathered. I knew they trusted Billy absolutely, and that his rapport with them was incredible.

They stayed with us for quite a time, all talking to Billy in their own individual ways. I was struck by the fact that those who were natural enemies seemed to be getting on extremely well together. Even the owl appeared to be casting loving glances at the mice and small birds who were present in abundance.

But I could not help but think, though, that like some humans he wore two faces, and that by nightfall, his benevolent attitude towards those present would change, certainly not for the better, for he, like the rest of them, had to eat. Nevertheless, they all seemed to be enjoying each other's company. I knew they were all living for the moment and was also determined to enjoy every minute of it. How I wished this outstanding, beautiful experience could go on for ever, but it was not to be for I saw Billy's spirit friends and my own drawing close to us.

Gradually, all the woodland animals took their leave of us. The birds fluttered and flew off, singing as loudly as they could. The last one to go, the barn owl, hesitated for a few seconds after moving up along Billy's outstretched legs, then spread his wings and disappeared as silently and as swiftly as he had arrived. I watched him go until he was out of sight, and wondered if he felt hungry.

There was no need for me to question Billy this time. I had not imagined the remarkable events that had taken place, but witnessed everything. I had not fallen asleep! We continued to sit by the pond in silence, with our backs resting against the trees, when I noticed several dragonflies hovering over the water. I was hoping for a repeat performance of the day before, but this time they went about their daily business.

I also noticed near the edge of the water a lot of tiddlers darting about. As I wanted to repay Billy in some way for the pleasure and kindness he had given me, I thought it was a good idea to suggest to him that if he had a net and a jar I would catch a few tiddlers for him.

Dear Billy was horrified at the thought and of my offer, surprised that I should suggest such a thing to him. I then realised – I should have known before – that he could not bear any creature, water species or otherwise, to be taken out of its natural habitat. I knew he was right, and made a solemn promise to myself that when I returned home there would be no more tiddler fishing by me and the kids when they all lined up with their tins and jars at the Serpentine in Hyde Park. I seemed to be luckier than most at catching the little fish. Therefore, it was expected of me to catch them for my little friends, but after being in Billy's company I was ashamed at what I had done, and determined that my fishing days were over. Needless to say, I did not inform Billy of my fishy activities. On second thoughts, though, I'm sure he must have known.

However, Billy and I remained firm friends. As it was close to mid-day, we had to leave the woods to have a meal. I was being so well fed I was starting to put on a little weight.

Billy called for me later. It was such a beautiful day; so far we had been blessed with warm, sunny days. After a short walk we stopped by a garden. Billy stood quietly and gave a soft low whistle. After a second or two, a large toad hopped towards him. Billy picked him up, kissed him, spoke to him and handed him to me. I was intrigued by the beautiful markings on the toad, thrilled to bits to be allowed to hold him, especially as I had never seen a live one before!

I remember thinking what a wonderful life Billy had to be able to live in the country. I wished my mum and dad could have been with me to see all that I had seen. Billy gently placed his toad friend under some leaves in the garden. We continued our walk along the lanes until we came to a large white gate with fields beyond. Billy opened the gate. We went into one field ablaze with buttercups, poppies, cornflowers and other wild flowers, all dancing gently in the breeze. Billy named them all for me.

We were not alone for coming towards us were a group of spirit friends bringing with them spirit children, all laughing as they ran towards us in greeting, such a delightful, happy moment.

I had helped myself to a few buttercups and poppies, and noticed that the spirit friends and the children were not picking the flowers. Neither was Billy. I felt self-conscious, once again, that I was not doing the right thing. Billy said to me: "Irene, these flowers and all plants have their own lives to lead for they are very alive. They are living. All have their own particular part to play in the plan of the universe as a whole. When you pick the flowers, you have reduced part of their life span."

Yes indeed, I was ignorant of such matters, but thinking over Billy's words, they made sense to me. How wise he was. One of Billy's spirit lady friends stepped out of the group and said to him, "You must not forget the frogs!" Then we all moved further across the fields where we came upon, to me, a natural pond, compared to the other one. It seemed quite small, but was bounding with life and activity.

I noticed all the spirit friends, including the children, were gradually moving away from us, fading away into a white mist which I was able to see clearly, even though the sun was shining brilliantly and it was very warm.

Billy whispered to me to sit down and make myself comfortable. There were no trees by the pond to rest against, but I did not mind as I was eagerly looking forward to what was going to happen next.

We sat close together upright, side by side with our legs outstretched. Billy closed his eyes for a few minutes. Then he spoke softly to me, saying: "Irene, look at the water. Do not move." Nothing happened for quite a while, then suddenly I saw a frog leap out of the water. He was in the middle of the pond. Then he dived back in. Shortly after, a few more repeated the same performance. They were leaping in numbers, two up, two down, alternately; three up, three down, and so on until there were many taking part. I was fascinated. Come to think of it now, it was like a ballet. I called it, "The Ballet of the Green Frogs." The timing and movements were perfect. Thinking of this event now, I would not be surprised if there had been a frog choreographer directing them behind the scenes.

Suddenly, one frog after another leapt – in single file – from the pond onto Billy's lap, then off again back into the pond. It seemed to me as though each one greeted Billy in his own individual way.

By this time, the spirit children had returned, quite a lot in number, and were standing behind Billy and myself, watching the performance of the frogs.

I watched them as they gradually returned to the water. Billy stated, "Keep still Irene for my friends have not finished their display yet."

The spirit children, some quite small, started to sing very softly. There were no words, but they created a melody by singing notes. Billy joined in with them. He had obviously sung with them. I am a lover of music, but have never heard since such beautiful music. It was indeed out of this world – and that is not a pun!

As the singing continued, the frogs suddenly popped their heads above the water. Thinking back, they had probably received a "briefing" from their choreographer! They then leapt out in small groups and hopped all over

Billy's lap and legs, and mine as well. Backwards and forwards they went, as though they were playing a game of tag.

It was so lovely to feel these little creatures jumping onto me. I was tickled pink because I knew they trusted me. How nice it would be, I thought, when I returned home if I could talk to my dear mum and dad about "The Ballet of the Green Frogs," and all that was happening to me, during my holiday with Billy, but I knew it would be impossible. They always found it hard to listen to my accounts of friendship with my spirit friends, let alone the performance of the frogs! Nevertheless, I would have loved to have shared my holiday experiences with them.

It was time for the ballet to draw to a close. One of the little spirit children said, "We must now take our leave of you for the time being." I watched them gradually fade away.

And the frogs? They stopped for a moment or two to form a circle around Billy and me, croaked in farewell, then returned whence they came. I asked Billy how often the frogs performed like that for him. "Only on rare and special occasions," he replied. Strange as it may seem, for the rest of the time – we spent about three hours talking by the pond – we did not see a single frog. Obviously their work for us and for the day was done. How I enjoyed every minute and being in their company.

The following day we roamed around the fields where Billy showed me the plant life. He had great knowledge of the names of all them, including the trees and the weeds. I noticed that wherever just the two of us went, many rabbits would come out and run around us, but they stayed away under cover if we were with a group of boys and girls. Billy certainly had that certain something.

My holiday was almost at an end. The time had gone so quickly, too fast for my liking. The day before I was due to return home, we paid my last visit to the woods. It was getting dark. Billy wanted to show me his friends, the foxes, who, odd as it may seem, appeared to be waiting for us.

As we drew close to them, the whole family were there. The dog fox and the vixen stepped forward and rubbed their heads against Billy's legs in greeting for quite a few minutes. They seemed to look up at Billy adoringly as they let him stroke them.

They also allowed Billy to pick up two young ones. Obviously, the foxes had met Billy many times to be on such friendly terms. For a while they stood looking at me with some suspicion. Then they all took their leave of us.

Then Billy and I went on to the badgers' sett. Billy said they were always very cautious friends, but hoped that as it was going to be my last night in Wiltshire, they would come out to greet me. Billy explained he always had a feeling his badger friends thought twice before making any decisions.

We did indeed wait for a very long time. Sitting quietly, I whispered to Billy, "I don't think they want to come to say 'Hello' to us." He replied: "Yes, they are going to. They are just making sure they will be all right. I can hear them talking."

I was astonished for I could not hear a thing, only the scuttle of a woodland animal, or the snapping of a twig. We were some distance away from the sett.

I whispered to Billy how was it possible for him to hear the badgers talking? He whispered back: "I hear them with my mind. They will be coming out in a moment or two." "That will be a blessing," I said, "because before long it will be too dark to see them."

No sooner had I spoken, when slowly they appeared out of the sett, but I noticed they kept a safe distance and made no attempt to move towards us. The little ones were peeping from the entrance. The parents were outside, and seemed to be guarding the family. The bigger one, which I thought was the father, stood up on his back legs. It looked as though he was sniffing the air, but his gaze was fixed on Billy who had his eyes shut, and appeared to be listening. I realised that Billy and the badger were holding a conversation by thought power.

After a few minutes had gone by, Billy stood up and said to me: "Irene, I know you will not be offended, but as the badgers do not know you, they will not come close to us. I am going to go over to them. You will be able to see them talking to me. The little ones are going to come out as well."

Several years afterwards I realised that at that moment of time I had witnessed a very remarkable demonstration of telepathy between Billy and the badger, but was far too young to appreciate the fact then.

Billy walked towards his friends. The little ones – three of them – excitedly came out of the sett and started to run round him in circles, while the parents tried to move as close to him as they could.

The father parent turned round many times to make sure I had not moved. He intended to keep a close watch on me.

I can still see that happy and joyous meeting as Billy lifted the little badgers up high, spoke to them one by one, and gently put them down. I remember his smiling face as they romped around him, with their parents standing sedately by watching the antics of their offspring. Like all good things, this moment of joy had come to an end.

The little badgers returned into the sett. Billy stood for some time talking to the parents, who allowed him to put his arms around them before they disappeared to join their family.

If only video cameras were available in those days all the lovely experiences I had witnessed could have been on record permanently. But that was not meant to be.

When it was time for us to leave the woods, it was quite dark. Billy explained to me he went on his own as often as he could to the fields and woods to his private world and to meet his beloved animal friends. Sometimes his spirit friends would accompany him. The ladies and gentleman were his spiritual teachers. They had taught him how to converse as one with all God's creatures, but he still had a great deal more to learn.

I thought after what I had seen and heard in his delightful company there could not be much more for him to learn and said so. He replied: "Irene, the universe, the other side of the curtain, is vast. Knowledge of communication with all that is living is there. You can open the doors, if you wish. Only you can decide for yourself." These wise words have remained with me throughout the years.

As we drew close to a very large oak tree, Billy said to me: "When you feel you need extra strength, always make your way to a tree and stand against it. You will feel the healing energy within it." He took my hand and placed it against the tree. I remember the tingling sensation I felt as I touched it.

As we continued on our way out of the woods, I started to feel a deep sense of sadness and could only think it was because my holiday with Billy was nearly over, but I was soon to discover that was not the real reason.

Suddenly Billy stopped walking, turned round to face me and held both of my hands. I instinctively felt I did not want to hear what he was going to say to me.

We stood looking at each other for a few moments. Then Billy quietly said to me, "Irene, you know that I am going to die young?" I could not believe what I was hearing and replied, "You must be mistaken, Billy." I was very shaken and deeply upset.

I asked him how he knew. He said: "My spirit friends have told me I will be leaving here to live with them. My stay on earth is only to be for a short time. I shall be called 'home' when I am thirteen years old."

Very nearly to tears – although I knew tears were not necessary, as Billy would live on anyway – I said to him: "You look very well, Billy. What is wrong that will cause you to die?"

Billy explained he had a disease called "Sleeping Sickness." Doctors had told his mother there was nothing they could do to help him.

Billy continued, "As you know, Irene, I shall be quite all right because it is only my body that will die, not me!" What a courageous little boy he was, speaking so calmly of his transition to the Higher Life. I knew how much he was looking forward to it in the knowledge that his earth journey – albeit a short one – and his "work" were coming to an end.

Billy went on to say that we would not meet again in this world, but we would see each other in the world of the spirit, but many years would come and go before then. I wanted to know how I would find out when he had departed for the Higher Life.

Billy said I was not to worry about it: he would see that the matter would be brought to my notice in due course. We held hands. Billy walked with me to the house where I was staying. We kissed each other goodbye, both of us knowing within ourselves that the parting of the ways was only temporary.

That night I could not sleep in the very comfortable bed provided for me. I was restless and very disturbed. The lady of the house came to see if I was all right, and brought me a hot drink. She asked me if I had enjoyed my holiday and with a strange look at me stated, "How nice young Billy is." I sensed she knew of Billy's illness, but did not discuss him with her for there was no need. She then left the bedroom.

A few minutes afterwards, it lit up with a beautiful golden light. I knew my spirit friends were about to pay me a visit, which I very much welcomed. Sure enough, several came. One lady - she was quite young - sat on my bed, after we had all greeted each other in love. She said she wanted to talk to me about young Billy. She confirmed that God would call him home early in life. His time was indeed drawing to a close. I would know better by not grieving for him as I knew in time I would see him again. She was pleased I had enjoyed all the time I had spent with Billy, and by his work and teachings had learnt a great amount of spiritual knowledge and advancement regarding the communication with all of God's creatures.

My spirit friend continued her conversation by saying that Billy and I were very old friends who had travelled through the centuries on earth. We had from time to time worked together in helping mankind and had met again in this life, but only for a brief space of time.

I understood perfectly well what her words meant, and thanked her for the comfort she gave me.

Before she and the other friends left, she stood up, bent over, held my hands and looking right into my eyes said: "Little one, always remember your holiday with our beloved Billy. In years to come you will fully understand why everything Billy has shown you - he calls it his secret world - will stand you in good stead for your future work with the animal kingdom that lies ahead. We trust you will not throw aside all that which has been given to you. Always treasure the Gifts of the Spirit, such as Billy has done and will continue to do so. Billy has carried out in love and dedication our plans for you. He has given you good training, if only for a short time. We know it will be put to use in due course in our time – not yours – but only when you are ready."

After blessing me, my spirit friends gradually faded into the golden light, and finally disappeared. So did the light. My feeling of sadness for Billy and my restlessness had gone. I was tremendously spiritually uplifted and felt very calm within. I soon drifted into the sleep state.

When I awoke in the morning, I remembered clearly that Billy and I had been together during the night in the spirit world. We walked hand-in-hand in a very beautiful spirit garden, laughed and talked. What about? I had not a clue! Obviously my lessons were over, and so was his rôle as my teacher.

But I like to think that perhaps our visit to the spirit world was an added bonus for both of us. Billy had certainly earnt it!

I got up and got ready for my departure, hoping Billy would be at the station to see me off. After a very hearty breakfast, laden with food, sandwiches, etc, to sustain us on our journey back, all the kids and myself were taken to the railway station. I was sorry to see that Billy was not there. After all, he had said we would not meet again. His work with and for me was finished.

We all said our goodbyes with some reluctance. The other children (not so lucky as me) had enjoyed the holiday in their own way and were going home much fatter (including myself) than when they arrived. What a difference good food – and plenty of it – makes!

When I arrived home, I could not discuss my holiday with my dear parents for I was still overflowing with great joy, happiness and spiritual upliftment over what had taken place in Wiltshire. I knew if I started to talk about it, I would have ended up by disclosing everything in detail so caution kept me very quiet indeed, until I had quietened down and was able to talk about the normal happenings that one encounters when on holiday.

Some years afterwards, I started work in a dress shop. I happened to be walking along a street, and came across a neatly folded newspaper lying on the pavement. It did not appear to have been opened. It could have been the "Evening News," although I am not absolutely sure. I picked it up, thought no more about it, and took it home.

Much later in the evening, I remembered the paper and sat down to read it.

I came across a short article concerning a member of Billy's family, a son who was ill. The article went on to say that Mr. and Mrs. G. had previously lost a son called Billy at the young age of thirteen with "Sleeping Sickness."

Dear Billy had, after all, kept his promise to me. It had taken a long time, but what is time in the world of spirit? I sat quietly and sent out my thoughts of thanks to him. I knew he was aware of my thoughts, but did not see him. To the present day, I have not had even a glimpse of him. I shall see him again – at the right time.

Through many years I have tried to recreate the wonderful experiences I had with Billy, to date with no luck. I have sat in the garden and mentally spoken to the birds, and the insects, but have not had the chance to go into the woods. The nearest the birds ever got to me is when they see me going into the garden with food for them, then they fly over my head calling to each other that "Dinner is on the tables!" No way have they settled on me.

The friendly robins and blackbirds occasionally fly down when they see me digging and stay about a foot away. They quickly swoop in when they have spotted a worm or two, then fly off and return to wait for further titbits. As for the insects, my endeavours in offering them love and friendship have had no effect on them whatsoever!

A little while ago, I did spot a dragonfly in the front garden. Eager as I was in my attempts to make friends, it left me very disappointed for after a matter of minutes when I really thought I was making some headway and that the dragonfly was "listening," it suddenly took off and I haven't seen one since!

Years ago I came to realise, when thinking of Billy, that he was a very rare spirit indeed. He was, in fact, the true essence of spirit in action in a physical body.

He expressed so wonderfully the pure quality and depth of his spirituality by his remarkable, outstanding ability to communicate with all living creatures, creating an atmosphere of love and trust, whereby even those who were by nature natural enemies were able to enjoy each other's company in harmony, albeit for a short space of time.

Without doubt, Billy is a highly evolved soul, in the same

category, I do not hesitate to say, as St. Francis of Assisi. Speaking of him, I must include the following. Not so long ago, a gentleman thought he was developing some of the powers of St. Francis when a song thrush allowed him to stroke its feathers.

Indeed, the bird offered no resistance when he picked it up and held it in his hands. A friend quickly disillusioned him by saying: "Oh that is quite common at this time of the year when apple windfalls are fermenting on the ground. Many birds feed on the apples and often end up so tight they can't move, let alone fly!"

There will be those who are sceptical reading this, my true story. But as this book is about animals, I wanted to relate the mentioned experiences for people who are sincerely seeking the truths of the spirit. I trust they will share – to some degree – my happiness, pleasure and overwhelming joy that I had received by being in the treasured company of a young St. Francis of Assisi, Billy G. I take this opportunity to thank him for his kindness and patience in teaching me my lessons oh, so very long ago!

All over the globe, for some considerable time, highly evolved souls endowed with all the gifts of the Spirit have been reborn on the earth plane. All are potential St. Francis of Assisi's, hidden away in their own secret worlds, but developing so naturally their affinities and communications with all living things on the earth plane, preparing for their spiritual work that lies ahead.

The world is covered by darkness and evil created entirely by man. This dark age will govern for a long time to come. Providing that man had not wiped himself and all other living matter off the face of the earth beforehand, in due course, if given the opportunity and the world is ready and will accept them, these spiritually trained young souls will put on their cloaks of service to mankind and teach them how to love and converse by thought Power as one with all of God's creatures.

It is certainly not an impossibility. For I have seen the power of thought in action with several kingdoms of life and been given the courage to put pen to paper (come what may) for the benefit of others. I trust they will listen and digest my story. And I will simply say, "Please give it due thought."

Chapter 11

Animals Guided

THE Spirit always seem to guide to Herbie's owner's front door unloved and unwanted animals, and those that need to be taken in. Mrs. Pawlyn once said to me, "It looks as though they actually know where to come as I cannot - and will not - turn them away."

I got to know her very well during the following months, and could fully understand the dear spirit friends directed poor, neglected and ill treated animals to her pathway for Mrs. Pawlyn is a lady full of compassion and deep, abiding love for all creatures within the animal kingdom. Indeed, it is a great privilege just to talk with her. How sad it is that some other animal keepers do not possess her qualities. Great Britain is supposed to be a nation of animal lovers. Are we really?

However, I must not get carried away, so will return to the story of dear little Herbie, who, being a rescue dog, was able to knock at Mrs. Pawlyn's door.

When she brought him to us, he was able to walk, but suffering from a massive tumour in the head, making the shape of it abnormal. His left eye was obviously showing signs of the disease.

As we waited for Charlie to arrive, I listened to Mrs. Pawlyn. She said she could not bear to have Herbie put to sleep, as her vet advised. She would only agree to it if there were no other way of helping him. That was why she brought him to us, hoping that Herbie would receive healing help. She loved him very much, and could not have him put down just like that. For all that she had given him, he had more than repaid her by the joy, love, trust and companionship he had displayed.

As I looked at them both, I was struck by the everlasting love bond that existed between them. I knew it would continue when Herbie was called "home," as indeed he was going to be in due course through the tumour.

Herbie listened intently, and understood every word his mistress was saying. As he looked up pleadingly at me, I knew he was asking me to help Mrs. Pawlyn through her distress. I realised then this lovely little dog was not only psychically very advanced but spiritually too, and that he and Mrs. Pawlyn were extremely well matched together.

Charlie and Spot arrived. Spot immediately greeted Herbie by gently touching his head for a moment or two. They both had a lot in common. Herbie, like Spot, was a mongrel. Herbie's coat was black and white whilst Spot is all black with a white patch over his eye. Yes, they got on very well indeed during the healing sessions that followed.

Spot looked at Charlie, wondering when the healing was going to commence. "Soon," said Charlie. I went into trance for Charlie and heard him explain to Mrs. Pawlyn that he could not promise a cure for Herbie or even an improvement in his condition. He sincerely hoped Herbie would not have to be put down, but would do everything possible to stop all pain for him, whereby he could live out his life span on earth. When the time came for Herbie to leave his physical body, he would help him quietly to slip out of it without any distress to Herbie whatsoever. But it was early days; we were to wait and see what happened regarding the healing.

So the contact operational healing commenced. Charlie showed me many parts and organs of Herbie's body which were already infected with cancerous cells. Charlie said to me: "I think we can keep this little fellow on his feet, and without suffering. It is necessary to operate on the parent tumour here in his head."

I watched Charlie deftly working round the tumour with a milky substance. I asked him what he was doing. He replied: "I cannot remove this tumour for it has spread with branches like a tree, but I can render it numb, putting it to sleep for a limited amount of time to deaden the nerves. It is rather like when you go to your dentist and you have injections to prevent pain occurring. Herbie will feel like you do, a numbness, but whereas yours is only for a short time, Herbie's will be for a longer period. With the substance I am using, he will not suffer any pain."

Dear Charlie kept his word. After the operation, Herbie started to show signs of improvement and maintained good progress, but still attended regularly every week for healing. Always with a smile on his face, he greeted us all warmly. Often he would lay his head on one side onto our hands, and Spot, bless him, was always there to say "Hello" to him.

Mrs. Pawlyn told us how Herbie was enjoying his life. He was eating like a horse, had a lot of energy, enjoyed his walks, and would run to the door if she were a little late to remind her it was time for them to visit us!

We were very pleased to see that Mrs. Pawlyn was happy because her dearly loved companion was still on his feet, completely without pain, despite the tumour which had started to show itself externally in the eye.

Ten months had gone by since the day of Herbie's spirit operation, when Charlie came to me to say that Herbie's time on earth was drawing to a close. We would notice that his back legs would show signs of weakness, otherwise he could carry on enjoying his life just the same, and without discomfort.

In due course, Herbie's legs became weaker so Mrs. Pawlyn carried him into the centre. Naturally, she was very concerned regarding his welfare, but Charlie assured her he would look after Herbie. She thanked Charlie for the extension of time she had enjoyed with Herbie.

Herbie received more contact healing, but I knew he realised he was going to be called "home." Shortly afterwards, Charlie requested Mrs. Pawlyn to keep Herbie comfortable at home: she was not to worry about him as all would be well. She was very relaxed, knowing that Charlie would keep his previous promise to her, when she and Herbie had first come to our centre.

A few days later, it was a weekend. During the Sunday morning, I became aware of Herbie being around. Then I saw him smiling and wagging his tail at me for all he was worth. Naturally, being in the spirit world, he was completely free of the tumour. Suddenly he vanished.

I phoned Mrs. Pawlyn straight away to tell her of Herbie's visit – and she informed me that Herbie had passed quite peacefully out of his body a few hours earlier. He always slept at the side of her bed. Herbie, she said, just gave a little sigh and was gone with no pain or no trouble at all.

Charlie indeed had kept his promise to them both. I shall not forget Herbie for he was always smiling . . . and no doubt still is!

Sam Pawlyn

SAM, a lovely Greyhound bitch, is another well-loved member of Mrs. Pawlyn's family. Sam is also a rescued companion. But unfortunately she had been ill-treated by her previous owners. When Mrs. Pawlyn held out her arms to her, she had acquired, a year previously, a metal plate in her right shoulder.

Mrs. Pawlyn noticed that Sam was very uncomfortable with it. It seemed to put the shoulder out, then Sam would squeal with pain, hence her visit to us. I noticed she was very wary when walking and avoided putting pressure on her right paw.

Charlie looked at her and stated: "She is in pain. The plate has been expertly inserted by a veterinary surgeon because of a serious injury to Sam's shoulder. Since then, she has had a collision with a person and the plate has moved a little, causing the discomfort. The area around the plate has become extremely sore and painful. The plate needs a little adjustment. I will give healing around the surrounding muscle tissue."

After receiving contact healing, Sam responded very well, and was able to walk and move without squealing with pain. Sam attended the centre only twice, and to date, thanks be to Charlie, has maintained excellent progress, according to Mrs. Pawlyn.

Sammy Mackenzie

THE following is a letter kindly sent to "Psychic News" by Barbara Mackenzie.

"I felt I must write and tell you of the absent healing that was given to my little cat, Sammy, by Irene and Gerald Sowter and their spirit vet, Charlie Kemp.

"Sammy became ill during July with congestion of the lungs. Despite veterinary attention, this continued in various degrees, but never clearing up completely. Three days before my husband and I were due to go on holiday,

Sammy had a bad attack and could not breathe. He was given emergency veterinary treatment, which enabled him to breathe more easily, and antibiotics. The diagnosis was again severe congestion of the lungs and bronchial tubes.

"We took Sammy – who was still quite poorly – to the cattery on September 3, as we had arranged before hand. Their own vet came in on September 5, to see him, and declared that he was fit and healthy, and stopped the antibiotic treatment. On returning home, we took Sammy to our own vet, who confirmed this.

"Sammy's absent healing treatment was started on September 3 – and after only three days' healing was cured completely, after his suffering, discomfort and stress and various treatments since July.

"I have never had experience of spirit healing before. Our little cat continues to improve by eating with relish, plays happily and purrs constantly!"

Six years later, Sammy is still very well and enjoying his life to the full with no physical ailments at all.

Chapter 12

"Seek and ye shall find"

SADLY, it is impossible for the seeker of spiritual and psychic truths to obtain any knowledge, teaching, instruction, lectures, or even join a down-to-earth discussion group at any of Orthodox churches. Apart from certain members of the clergy who administer healing to the needy via the one-way system, though all roads lead to the same God, the seekers seek in vain. Unfortunately, to mention other subjects such as clairvoyance, clairaudience, transfiguration, trance, psychic art, automatic writing, apports and many other gifts of the Spirit is strictly taboo. Why?

Paul states in his first epistle to the Corinthians (chapter 12, verse 1.), "Now concerning spiritual gifts, brethren, I would not have you ignorant . . ." It is just a thought, but maybe in time, free, forward thinking people will be courageous enough to try to introduce the essence of spiritual truths within the walls of the holy sanctums on behalf of, and benefit for, the desperate parishioners.

However, to those who are out on a limb, wise counselling and sound advice regarding the mentioned subjects can be obtained from:

The Arthur Findlay College, Stansted Hall, Stansted Mountfitchet, Essex, tel: 0279 813636/7.

The Spiritualist Association of Great Britain, 33, Belgrave Square, London, SW1X 8QB. 071-235 3351.

The Greater World Christian Spiritualist Association, 3-5, Conway Street, London W1P 5HA. 071-436 7555.

The Institute of Spiritualist Mediums, for details contact General Secretary. Mrs Leslie James, 1, Jennings Close, Stevenage, Herts SG1 1SA.

Some details of Spiritualists' National Union churches and Christian Spiritualist churches appear in "Psychic News," 2, Tavistock Chambers, Bloomsbury Way, London WC1A 2SE. 071-405 3340.

The National Federation of Spiritual Healers, Old Manor

Farm Studio, Church Street, Sunbury-on-Thames, Middlesex. 0932 873164/5.

Our sanctuary is the Universal Healing Centre, 54, Hitchings Way, Reigate, Surrey. 0737 242853. Please enclose an SAE when writing. Whilst we make no charge for healing humans or animals, freewill donations are accepted.

A Conversation Overheard.

"Arthur's funeral is on Tuesday." "Was he dead then?" "No, they are taking him up the churchyard to see if he likes it!"